The Ecology of Money

The Ecology of Money

Debt, Growth, and Sustainability

Adrian Kuzminski

LEXINGTON BOOKS
Lanham • Boulder • New York • Toronto • Plymouth, UK

Published by Lexington Books
A wholly owned subsidiary of The Rowman & Littlefield Publishing Group, Inc.
4501 Forbes Boulevard, Suite 200, Lanham, Maryland 20706
www.rowman.com

10 Thornbury Road, Plymouth PL6 7PP, United Kingdom

Copyright © 2013 by Lexington Books

British Library Cataloguing in Publication Information Available

Library of Congress Cataloging-in-Publication Data

Library of Congress Cataloging-in Publication Data Available ISBN: 978-0-7391-7717-4 (cloth : alk. paper ISBN: 978-0-7391-7718-1 (electronic)

∞™ The paper used in this publication meets the minimum requirements of American National Standard for Information Sciences Permanence of Paper for Printed Library Materials, ANSI/NISO Z39.48-1992.

Printed in the United States of America

To the Memory of George McGuire

Contents

Introduction

This book argues that our ecological crisis is a consequence of the productive effort we must make to meet the demands of our financial system, and that this crisis is upon us since we no longer have the natural resources to sustain this effort.

The roots of this financial-economic dynamic lay far back, in the financial revolution of the seventeenth and eighteenth centuries in Europe which created our modern money and banking system, and which, this book argues, made the industrial revolution possible.

The financial revolution favored private credit over public credit. It gave the private banking system a legal monopoly over money creation through debt on which high rates of interest had to be paid. The Bank of England became the symbol of this "English system," as Alexander Hamilton called it, which was subsequently exported to America and most of the modern world.

Once key sectors of the economy came to depend on money borrowed continuously at usurious rates of interest, it became necessary to keep expanding economic output. The obligation to repay such debts is what forced modern economies into seemingly endless "growth." Traditional, steady-state, sustainable economies were rapidly displaced by economies relentlessly seeking out new markets, technologies, resources, and laborers, and the industrial revolution—what we call "modernity"—was born.

More than two centuries of economic "growth" have given us the miracle of the modern world, with all its astounding wealth and technology. That miracle has also exhausted our planet, which now staggers under the cumulative effects of resource depletion, pollution, overpopulation, and climate change. Insofar as the limits to growth have been reached, we can no longer hope to repay our debts, as in the past, by growing our way out of the crisis.

Although our "too big to fail" financial system has succeeded in transferring much of this excessive debt onto taxpayers, this has only postponed and likely intensified the final reckoning. We are further burdened by an increasingly dysfunctional political system—itself largely corrupted by the financial system—which is less and less responsive to the urgency of reform.

The now interwoven ecological and financial crisis will play itself out no matter what we do. Having looked back in history to the origins of our predicament, it is useful to look ahead as well to its resolution. What the survivors will need as they adjust to a dramatic downsizing and a return to sustainable economic practices is a financial system compatible with a steady-state, non-growth economy.

The outlines of such a system actually exist: they were developed by a nineteenth-century American financial theorist, Edward Kellogg, who proposed a decentralized system of low-interest credit creation through local public banks, where citizens could borrow on good collateral at low, nonusurious rates of interest fixed by law. Kellogg's system is updated here and offered as a model for financing a future sustainable economy.

A sustainable, steady-state economy, we should be clear, is not necessarily a static or primitive economy. To say that we can no longer tolerate exponential growth as we have known it is not to say that human ingenuity has no future, that profound innovations in human life are no longer possible, or that the vast store of scientific and technical knowledge born of the industrial revolution cannot be adapted to new circumstances.

The challenge of getting the most out of limited resources may itself lead to surprising and unanticipated consequences, and perhaps to new depths of self-awareness. And, unlikely as it now seems, human beings may, at some future point, leave the planet to discover vast new resources and colonize new worlds, leading to a resumption of dramatic growth.

Our immediate prospects, however, are more daunting. This book offers a sobering diagnosis of our general predicament, but it is by no means a fatal one. Human history has long swung between extremes—boom and bust, feast and famine, peace and war, the rise and fall of civilizations—and we have no reason to believe our era is exempt from that ancient dynamic. We are a resilient species, and the silver lining of any crisis has always been the opportunity to learn from one's mistakes, an opportunity perhaps not otherwise possible. Let's make the best of it.

This book is an outgrowth of an earlier work of mine, *Fixing the System: A History of Populism, Ancient & Modern*. Nineteenth-century American populists developed a profound critique of what has since become our dominant financial system. In their view, the undue concentrations of wealth and power which were coming to dominate American society in their day—and are even more conspicuous today—were due to an emerging system of privatized, usurious finance, which they called "the money power."

This populist critique of modern finance has largely been ignored since the political defeat of the populists in the 1890s. History, after all, is mostly written by the winners. Yet the populists, I believe, put their finger on the central mechanism by which wealth and power are concentrated by the few at the expense of the many. This mechanism, it turns out, has a longer and deeper history then even they realized. Privatized usurious credit lies, if this book is correct, at the heart of modernity itself, and is the key to its current crisis.

I have a few personal acknowledgements. One of them is to the late George McGuire, who brought to my attention the works of Edward Kellogg. I regret that we were never able to complete our pilgrimage to Kellogg's grave in Green-Wood cemetery in Brooklyn. I am indebted to the anonymous outside reader for Lexington Books for several useful suggestions. I am also grateful to my friends at Hartwick College, especially in the Philosophy and Religion Departments, who have provided me with a scholarly home while writing this and other works. Finally, I am deeply indebted to my family for their support, particularly to my wife and best editor, Antoinette Mendlow Kuzminski.

Chapter One

Growth and Money

This is a book about the relationship between money and nature, between financial systems and ecological sustainability. It offers a new historical account of the rise of modern society—which began with the industrial revolution—based on the reinvention of money as credit. I argue that the industrial revolution was precipitated by a preceding financial revolution which first developed in Holland and Britain in the seventeenth and eighteenth centuries, and was subsequently exported to the United States and much of the rest of the world. This financial revolution, itself preceded by a still earlier commercial revolution, was a revolution in credit, which was made much more widely available than at any time in history. As a result, individuals, governments, and corporations were able to access funds to utilize resources on a scale hitherto unimaginable, making possible in due course the untold wonders of the modern age. This unprecedented exponential growth of industrial production and the lifestyle of modernity as we know it would not have occurred, I argue, without the financial revolution which preceded it. The new availability of credit—*and in particular, as we shall see, credit with excess or usurious interest*—made it not only possible but *necessary* to insist upon steadily increasing production. The accompanying interest costs on loans—a contractual obligation—could not easily be evaded, so production had to be continually expanded to accommodate those costs; hence the modern compulsion to grow, no matter what.

The new financial instruments—public and private credit, national debt, bonds, money markets, fractional reserve banking, etc.,—made it not only possible but necessary to exploit resources and labor to create vast new wealth. This new ability, indeed compulsion, to go into debt as a means for realizing a vast range of desires was initially an enormous boon for humankind. Much of humanity—especially in the developed countries, but else-

1

where as well—benefited beyond anyone's wildest dreams. Just compare material life today across much of the world to that of 250 years ago. Yet this new credit-based growth economy was fatally compromised from the start. The eco-crises we face today is largely the result of the very rapid, unprecedented expansion of industrial production over the last two hundred years. As a result, we have been brought to the brink of global catastrophe, manifest in the symptoms of polluting emissions, climate change, environmental degradation, ecological disruption, severe weather, species extinctions, resource depletion, population stress, disparities of incomes and assets, and potential social breakdown.

The key difficulty—it cannot be overemphasized—was that credit was made available by the financial revolution, but only on condition of excessive or usurious interest rates. A excessive or usurious rate, as we shall see in detail, is one which demands in repayment more than the replacement value of the loan. To put it another way: If it takes more net value to repay a loan than the net value captured by that loan in the first place, including all the normal costs of risk, inconvenience, etc., then repayment is excessive or usurious. Private institutions, beginning with the Bank of England in the early eighteenth century, achieved not only effective control over national monetary systems, allowing them to dominate national finance in the interests of creditors and other investors, but they did so while charging excessive rates of interest. They were able to create and lend money to governments and the public at high rates, thereby stimulating production, while keeping disproportionate profits for their investors. The new usurious credit system and the usurious economy it created forced, I shall try to show, the unprecedented leap in productivity we call the industrial revolution.

Traditional subsistence and early commercial economies before the industrial revolution were largely reciprocal in nature—goods and services were traded most of the time by most people for more or less equivalent values. Such growth as occurred was slow and incremental, and depended mostly on serendipitous technological innovations or resource discoveries (the waterwheel, the windmill, the stirrup, the compass, gunpowder, new trade routes, land and gold in the New World, etc.). Up until the nineteenth century subsistence economies were the rule; economic life everywhere was constrained by the need to operate almost entirely on renewable resources. But once the bulk of productive enterprise—both agriculture and manufacturing—came to be financed by money borrowed at usurious rates of interest, then a powerful motivation, hitherto lacking, was built into the heart of the economic system: the need not only to pay back the borrowed money, but to expand production sufficiently to pay back the extra interest now demanded on the principal.

The price of borrowing became central to economic activity. Bill Gross, bond manager at PIMCO (Pacific Investment Management Company), one of the largest and most important funds of recent decades, put it this way: "The cost of credit, the interest rate [on a benchmark bond], ultimately determines the value of stocks, homes, all asset classes."[1] Producers relying on loans with interest in a growth economy can no longer be content with equivalent exchanges. Expectations of reciprocity are replaced by the necessity of gain, or profit, on a continuing basis. Producers are increasingly compelled to find ways of getting more back than they give out since the failure to do so means the triumph, at their expense, of competitors who will. The legalization of usury in the wake of the Protestant reformation in Europe—combined with other innovations comprising no less than a financial revolution—unleashed an explosion of debt-financing which largely destroyed most older patterns of reciprocity in human relations, and became the key factor driving the industrial revolution and modern civilization—thereby promoting the excessive "growth" of human society, and leading us to our current plight of ecological overshoot.

The ability of creditors to take profits for themselves led from the beginning to new concentrations of wealth and power in the hands of a new financial elite. "The monied interest" was a phrase in circulation as early as the 1690s in Britain.[2] Then as now the monied interests were a small minority. There were ten or eleven thousand public creditors in Britain in 1709, and fifty to sixty thousand by the 1750s.[3] They were never a large group. "By the early nineteenth century," writes financial historian Niall Ferguson, "the number of British bondholders may have been fewer than 250,000, barely 2 percent of the population. Yet their wealth was more than double the entire national income of the United Kingdom."[4] The resulting inequalities were by and large tolerated—reactionary, populist, socialist, and progressive resistance over decades, even centuries, notwithstanding—as long as economic growth produced a growing economic pie for creditors and debtors alike to divide up. In the heyday of the industrial revolution—from the early nineteenth to the late twentieth centuries—a large debt burden could be absorbed and discharged by continued economic growth. Britain at the end of the Napoleonic wars found itself carrying a debt burden more than double the size of her economy—comparable to current sovereign debts. Yet the astonishing explosion of industrial production in the decades which followed, along with the cessation of military expenditures associated with the Napoleonic wars, allowed this debt to be absorbed and discharged, leaving room to issue more new debt on an ongoing basis. Debtors repaying even usurious loans generally stood to benefit from a steadily growing economy. This seemingly endless growth has been the touchstone of the modern economy for over 200 years. Even today, in spite of the eco-crisis and the disruptions following the crash of 2008, it is still widely presumed by most commentators that economic growth can be resumed. Calls for the resumption of "growth" remain a virtually unquestioned mantra of the mainstream media and contemporary political discourse.

By the late twentieth century, however, it had become apparent to some observers that economic growth was beginning to stall.[5] Resource depletion—particularly of fossil fuels—along with pollution, climate change, and population increases all called further economic growth into question. The industrial revolution unleashed by the invention of usurious credit began to come up against increasingly intractable limits, the most fundamental of which was energy. The compulsion to produce driven by the modern debt-and-interest financial system quickly depleted ready energy sources such as wood, and so from early on led to an intense search for new sources of energy. The result was the industrial development of fossil fuels, first coal and then oil. These turned out, once discovered and put to use, to be extraordinarily potent—unlike anything before them; they also had the advantage of being obtained relatively easily and cheaply. That allowed for unprecedented levels of production resulting in the industrial cornucopia we know today as modern consumer society.

Unfortunately the dependence of modern economies on fossil fuels—which by most measures make up as much as 80 percent of the energy consumed in the United States and other economically advanced countries—turned out to be a dependence on a non-renewable resource. Unless some equivalent substitute for these fuels can be found—a possibility yet to be realized as this is written—a severe energy shortfall looms before us all. The discovery of shale gas and oil reserves may stave this off for a time, but the expensive technologies, serious environmental harms, and more rapid depletion rates which come with shale gas and oil ensures that this non-renewable energy source will remain a stop-gap, not a permanent solution. To compound matters further, the availability of cheap energy allowed for the exploitation to the point of exhaustion of other finite resources—soils, forests, fresh water, fisheries, minerals, etc. The current growth of population insured that the demands on these increasingly scare resources would only increase. The side-effects of pollution of air, water, and land have added enormous further costs to industrialization—so-called "externalities" not included in conventional business bookkeeping but borne by society and the environment. This ecological and resource crisis portends not only the end of economic growth, but a drastic downsizing of a significantly overextended economy, and therefore of society itself. The economic downsizing such a shortfall would trigger might well portend significant social breakdown: perhaps the kind of collapse recently popularized by authors like Jared Dimond and Dmitry Orlov. The worst case scenarios envision social chaos, political anarchy, general mayhem, and die-off. The film *The Road*, based on the novel by Cormac McCarthy, captures this vision in its portrayal of the struggle of a few survivors reduced to a prehistoric level of hunting and gathering among the debris left by our fallen civilization.

The gloomy views of the radical ecologists are rooted in the idea of carrying capacity, developed as long ago as 1863 by the German scientist, Justus von Liebig. As restated by a classic early ecologist, William R. Catton, Jr., "carrying capacity is . . . limited not just by food supply, but potentially by *any* substance or circumstance that is indispensable but inadequate. The fundamental principle is this: whatever necessity is least abundantly available (relative to per capita requirements) sets an environment's carrying capacity."[6] For the pre-modern world that substance was food; for the modern world that substance is the fossil fuel on which industrial food production itself now depends. Renewable resources (fisheries, forests, croplands, etc.) are subject to Liebig's principle as well, but if they are preserved they hold the promise of producing a limited but perpetual supply of the materials in question. Non-renewable fossil fuels, by contrast, have allowed overshoot by supporting temporarily a much larger population than would otherwise have been possible.

We might think of global fossil fuel overshoot as similar to the localized Irish potato overshoot of the 1840s. In that case, the least available necessary resource was the potato, a food staple which had become essential to supporting a rapidly increasing population in Ireland of more than eight million people. With the arrival of the potato blight that least abundant supporting resource was suddenly removed, resulting in massive famine and an eventual reduction of Ireland's population down to two million. Fossil fuels may not disappear overnight, as did the Irish potato, but—lacking an adequate substitute in the face of increasing dependence and scarcity—some kind of serious downsizing is what ecological science predicts. The global rather than local nature of the fossil fuel crisis suggests that it will be much harder to escape. The Irish could immigrate to America; we cannot yet emigrate to another planet.

Once fossil fuels begin to be drawn down there is no provision, as things stand now, for sustaining our current population. There is no need to rehearse here the well-known exponential growth curve of population since the industrial revolution. That growth could not have occurred without the use of fossil fuels for energy and fertilizer. Instead of a few million hunters and gatherers predating the agricultural revolution, or the billion or so people at the dawn on the industrial revolution around 1800, we now have over seven billion people on the planet and counting, all dependent on the hunting and gathering not of plants and animals, but of fossil fuels. Catton estimates that it would take ten additional earths to support the four billion or so population of his day—the 1980s—on renewable resources.[7] Today's greater population presumably would require even more extra earths to sustain it. Various calcu-

lations of the earth's carrying capacity are available; most of them continue
to be more optimistic than Catton and the radical ecologists.

An example of mainstream discussion of carrying capacity is to be found
in Joel E. Cohen's *How Many People Can the Earth Support?* Cohen's work
is typical in its confidence that as yet undiscovered technologies will—if
pressed by scarcity of vanishing resources, as in the past—yet again provide
new substitutes for those resources. This act of faith allows him to presume
that substitutes will be found for fossil fuels, our least abundant necessity,
avoiding energy drawdown. It allows him to dismiss Liebig's law, and entertain inflated calculations of carrying capacity. In his words:

> The population size set by Liebig's law of the minimum does not really apply
> to human populations . . . because the human population is not homogeneous
> in its resource requirements, and because the environment varies enough in
> time and place to invoke different limiting factors at different times and places,
> and because interactions among limiting factors (sometimes appearing as eco-
> nomic substitutions) are not small enough to neglect, and because the time
> interval over which the carrying capacity is to be estimated is not short enough
> to justify the neglect of adaptive economic, technological and cultural re-
> sponses.[8]

Unfortunately, none of these reasons hold up. The human population across
the world today—outside of more or less isolated rural areas in third world
countries where subsistence economies persist—is indeed homogeneous in
its dependence on at least one resource, fossil fuels, for which no adequate
replacement is currently available. No variation in the environment invoking
"different limiting factors" which might alleviate some of the dependency on
fossil fuel consumption is apparent with regard to mass consumption of fossil
fuels. Insofar as there are relevant environmental changes, they are mostly
negative (such as the increase in atmospheric CO_2 and methane), and are
themselves largely the result of fossil fuel production and consumption. And
while "economic substitutions" are possible in theory—solar power is perhaps the most promising—so far they remain unavailable on a scale large
enough, cheap enough, and renewable enough to be sustaining. Even if an
adequate, clean, renewable, and cheap source of energy were made available,
we would still face the limits of other finite non-energy resources, such as
fisheries, forests, croplands, water, air, minerals, and metals, among many
others. The point is that our current financial-economic system has rapidly
pushed us beyond these resource limits, and that sooner or later we will have
to replace that system, at least on this planet, with one respectful of those
limits if we are to have any hope of stabilizing the situation. By all indications, infinite growth on a finite planet—a goal still widely proclaimed—is
self-defeating in the long run, and that long run may have arrived.

How narrow the neck of the bottle through which we must pass, given the coming downsizing, remains to be seen. This work does not address the immediate challenge of downsizing, to whose seeming inevitability our best evidence points; that will have to be endured as it plays itself out. What this book argues in subsequent chapters, however, is that the exponential growth of human societies since the eighteenth century has been compelled not simply by technological innovation or unique social or political factors, as most historians and commentators presume, but on a deeper level by something quite different: the legal obligation of borrowers to produce goods and services well beyond their own needs and desires in order to pay exponential rates of interest on their loans. Exponential rates are usurious rates: they force borrowers, and in modern times that means the economy generally, to expand production beyond non-exponential or sustainable levels, leading to boom and bust, overshoot and collapse.[9] If we are ever to have a sustainable economy, we will have to have a non-usurious financial system.

If this analysis is correct, we can no longer support an infinitely expanding debt because we no longer can count on an infinitely expanding economy to pay off that debt. Coming up against limited resources and other impediments to economic growth is not a new human experience, though in the past it has always been a local not a global phenomenon. In a pattern continually replayed during the several millennia of pre-industrial, agrarian societies, once no more new lands were readily available to bring under cultivation, nor no more new technologies (the plow, the waterwheel, the windmill, etc.) to deploy, the abundance of a growth phase disappeared as population caught up with resources, bringing things back to a subsistence level; after that, expansion might resume, but only if new resources and techniques could be found. Traditional subsistence agrarian societies had to operate within the constraints of renewable energy sources, ensuring that booms and busts would be relatively confined and repetitive, rather than cumulative and globally threatening.

A subsistence society is a sustainable society, we should be clear, but not necessarily an impoverished one. The agrarian-based economic cycle had its ups as well as its downs, and its oscillating dynamic is perhaps best captured by Thomas Malthus's conflict between population and resources. "Subsistence" can mean not just the bare bones of survival, but also what we would find in a country whose resources are "just equal," as Malthus puts it, "to the easy support of its inhabitants."[10] The challenge in this context was to maintain a measure of prosperity by keeping down population relative to resources. This is a key insight into sustainability, and we might consider Malthus to be the first philosopher of sustainability and one of the earliest and most trenchant critics of the idea of "growth." The industrial revolution, by contrast, was the game-changer which overthrow traditional subsistence; it gave us, for the first time in history, seemingly limitless economic growth on a vast scale, allowing us to transform our physical surroundings through science and technology far beyond anyone's expectations. In recent decades, however, as the economy has reached the limits of resource exploitation, as we have used up our stored natural capital in the earth, high interest rates have become increasingly difficult to justify. The long binge of living beyond our means, of consuming our natural capital without replacing it, has become ever more difficult to continue. As the "growth" economy today appears more and more unsustainable, we face the challenge of relearning to live within our means on renewable resources.

With the brakes now applied to economic growth worldwide, we are left with an enormous and still increasing debt burden which we cannot hope to discharge. The total debt burden of the United States government, for instance, including unfunded mandates, stands at something over $60 trillion, which is roughly 500 percent of GDP. Beyond this there are the debt burdens of state and local governments, corporations, and private individuals. Most other developed countries have comparable debt burdens. This is an unprecedented world-historical situation. Previous large debt overshoots were either absorbed by subsequent economic growth—like Britain's after the Napoleonic wars—or else ended in collapse. These earlier collapses, however, most notable the Great Depression, along with other earlier depressions and panics, were largely temporary affairs until the credit system of the day, which had seized up with an excess of bad loans, was able to restart after liquidation with new lenders finding new creditors exploiting new economic opportunities.

Today, without underlying opportunities for growth, we face the prospect of large-scale liquidation in the wake of the great crash of 2008; this outcome has been temporarily forestalled, however, by continual infusions of new credit (TARP funds, corporate bailouts, quantitative easing by central banks, etc.). The bankruptcies and heavy losses which should have been inflicted on the economy in the normal course of events were initially avoided, but the economy has not recovered from the crash. The new money created by these loans—in the United States mostly from the Federal Reserve lending to "too big to fail" banks—has largely been unable to find productive investment outlets; as a result, the new money has largely been held in reserve by those banks, or put into the stock market speculation. The Federal Reserve has recently announced indefinite quantitative easing, that is, open-ended lending to the banking system in hopes of keeping the economic system afloat.

When the overall debt burden is too great for the economy to sustain, there are two options: collapse or inflation. The great example of the former is the worldwide Great Depression of the 1930s; the great example of the latter is the hyperinflation of the Weimar Republic in Germany in the 1920s. Collapse means the acceptance of bankruptcies, unemployment, and a general economic retrenchment. In a collapse, the liquidation or deleveraging of debts reduces the money supply, resulting in a depreciated or stronger currency. Inflation on the other hand avoids collapse by injecting more money into the system, keeping afloat otherwise insolvent business enterprises through cash infusions. The idea is to postpone the day of reckoning, with the hope that somehow in the meantime economic growth will resume so that the new debt burden can eventually be discharged, as so often in the past, with insolvent enterprises becoming solvent once more, and new ones starting up. Much of current economic debate in the United States and around the world today focus on whether to continue financial injections—as argued most forcefully by economist Paul Krugman in his *New York Times* columns, or whether to bite the bullet and accept economic austerity—the course of action advocated by some conservatives and pursued to a somewhat greater degree in the Eurozone countries than in the United States.

How is money injected into the system in hopes of keeping it going? Normally, the government borrows money by selling bonds, which are either purchased by brokers, usually associated with commercial banks, or purchased directly by individuals, as in the case of war bonds or savings bonds. By buying or selling government bonds to commercial banks in sufficient quantity, a central bank (such as the Federal Reserve in the United States) can increase or decrease the amount of loans outstanding, and thereby the amount of money in circulation. Most money, after all, is created primarily through lending by commercial banks to the public, but the rate of lending is normally governed by the central bank since commercial banks have to keep minimal reserves on hand, and so must adjust their lending (more or less) in response to whether the central bank is buying or selling government bonds insofar as those bonds are the principal content of the reserves commercial banks must hold. If there are not enough buyers of government bonds from the public or foreigners, the central bank simply steps in and monetizes the debt: in other words, the central bank buys the excess issue of bonds to prop up the bond market. As a result, more money is injected into the system than current market forces would normally support. Money thus injected—on a huge scale in the United States since the crash of 2008, by some estimates amounting to more than $13 trillion—is done so in hopes of jumpstarting economic growth sufficiently to absorb the new debt. The problem arises when such growth fails to materialize, or is inadequate to do the job.

It is instructive to examine what is perhaps the best historical case study illustrating this debt dilemma, namely, the case of Weimar Germany and its infamous hyperinflation of the early 1920s.[11] Like the developed world today, Germany in the aftermath of the First World War found itself with an enormous debt burden it had no realistic hope of discharging. Like the United States today, Germany had little appetite for austerity, preferring instead to create even more debt to stave off collapse. The strategy of inflating the currency can be very effective in the short run for avoiding an economic downturn, and so is hard to resist. In the German situation, inflation was surprisingly successful for a time in maintaining a booming economy and more or less full employment. German products, underwritten by relatively cheap energy costs and by the fact that German industry was largely spared the ravages of World War I, were internationally competitive, and her exports were helped by the depreciation of the mark vis-à-vis other currencies.

German labor unions were strong, and able, through pressure and strikes, to secure pay raises for workers somewhat commensurate with inflation in the early and middling stages of the inflation. Debtors with mortgages found they could pay them off cheaply. The stock market went up. The post-war socialist governments expanded social welfare programs, adding to the demand for money. German industrialists, led by Hugo Stinnes (who put together a vast industrial conglomerate), favored the inflationary policy which averted recession. Moreover, German inflation did not unfold suddenly, but began during World War I when the decision was made not to increase taxes to fund the war effort (in contrast to Britain and France) but to spare the public and instead to inflate the currency by floating ever more debt. After the war the specter of reparations to the Allies complicated the situation. Though reparations in themselves—about a third of the overall German debt—were probably not decisive in fueling inflation, they quickly became a political sticking point and bogeyman, providing a further motive to continue already existing inflationary policies. The situation was further exacerbated by the frugal temperament of German society, with its ethic of savings which left many highly vulnerable to inflation. Those who suffered were largely those on fixed incomes, including public officials, bureaucrats, academics, pensioners, and *rentiers*.

By 1923, however, the moderate inflation of the war and post-war years turned into out-of-control hyperinflation. In the end, nearly everyone—excepting some industrialists, large landowners, speculators, and financial insiders—was financially ruined. In Weimar Germany there was no political will to stop the inflation until it was too late. The inflation ended only with the complete worthlessness of the German mark.[12] In this kind of financial system—under which, in essentials, we still live today—short-terms gains by a controlling coalition of special interests can fatally undermine the public good. Monetary policy in Germany in the 1920s—as in most developed countries before and since, including the United States today—remained largely unaccountable to the public. A small group of public officials influenced by powerful industrialists were able to drive Germany into financial catastrophe.

Germany in the 1920s succumbed to hyperinflation even though it did not face the preeminent problem of today: global resource depletion and environmental degradation. Raw materials were relatively plentiful, and once the currency collapsed the ingredients for resuming economic growth with a new currency were still available. In the United States and the leading industrial powers today, however, the option of picking up the pieces after a financial collapse appears no longer to be present, and certainly not to the same extent. Everything we know about the eco-crisis tells us that we should no longer expect the kind of eventual recovery which everyone used to take for granted. Nonetheless, just as in Germany, the desire today of the powers that be to avoid an economic collapse continues. The dollar today is worth but a small fraction of what it was just a generation ago; its value has steadily eroded over decades, and the everyday reality of increasing costs for energy and other resources belies even the still moderate inflation rates which are officially reported. We are on the same road the Germans took, and for many of the same reasons—including, above all, a reluctance to suffer severe economic pain, with its destabilizing political implications. Our other option— liquidation and collapse—is hardly more palatable. Our choices are daunting at best.

This analysis does not suggest optimism about any reform of the financial and monetary system adequate to evade the two drastic options before us: inflation and the threat of hyperinflation and financial meltdown on the one hand, and a default on debts leading to deflation and economic collapse on the other hand, marked by widespread liquidation and unemployment. It may be the case that monetizing the debt can be carried on for quite some time, but in the absence of any real solution to the eco-crisis the inflow of dollars into the economy will not be able to restart economic growth, returning us to our dilemma. The United States today, unlike Germany in the 1920s, lacks a strong organized working class which can make sure through unions and strikes, if necessary, that its share of national income more or less keeps pace with inflation. As a result, the benefits of inflation go disproportionately to a narrow band of the upper class—the notorious one percent. As long as most of the inflated money remains "on the sidelines" in bank accounts or equities or corporate balance sheets and does not enter the everyday economy, inflation will be moderate as far as the pubic is concerned. But the result over time will be a steady transfer of wealth to the one percent, with the relative impoverishment of everyone else. On this scenario, if the elites can manage it, a slow economic decline might be managed sufficiently to preserve and consolidate their wealth and power in an impoverished world. On the other hand, the credit burden may spark a crisis and collapse.

The underlying problem—the usurious credit system which underlies our economic system—will not easily be solved; indeed, it seems likely that it might be replaced only if there is a final crash dramatic and sufficient enough to discredit it in the eyes of the public. Unless there is a clear alternative available, however, the current system with all its flaws may eventually be reconstituted, or perhaps something even worse may replace it. We should be clear that our financial system—almost universally taken for granted—is not the only possible one, that it was created only relatively recently, that it serves the interests of the few not the many, and that there are other monetary and financial systems worth taking seriously. In the following chapters I outline the background of the usurious credit system and trace its birth to the financial revolution of the seventeenth and eighteenth centuries in Holland and Britain. I try to show how this devilish and dynamic financial system created the key incentives for economic growth resulting in the industrial revolution, and indeed in modernity itself, and how this has led to our current crisis.

But an accurate analysis of our dilemma, necessary as it is, is not enough. We also need a clear picture of what a non-usurious financial system appropriate to a steady-state rather than growth economy might look like. In chapter seven, I outline such a system in some detail. Let me anticipate that discussion here. It turns out that many of the implications of the usurious economy were recognized by Edward Kellogg, a little known American monetary theorist of the early nineteenth century. His work provides the most thought-out model for a sustainable monetary and economic system which this author has found. Kellogg developed in considerable detail an alternative monetary scheme, one which would replace the privatized, centralized financial system of his day (and ours) with a public, decentralized financial system. Credit would be available at sustainable not extortionary rates of interest. A sustainable rate of interest, as we shall see, turns out to be about one percent per year. Since resources which are consumed have to be replenished, it turns out that the rate of reinvestment necessary to continually replenish and stabilize an economy—without its growing or shrinking—is about one percent per year, which corresponds to the consumption cycle of a typical human lifetime. A one percent interest rate on credit is the mechanism which ensures that this replenishment—and thereby a steady-state economy—can be financed without the compulsion to "grow." Any rate beyond that can be considered usurious.

His most important work, *A New Monetary System*, was published posthumously in 1861. Kellogg helped inspire the financial and monetary policies of the American populist movement in its heyday after the Civil War. The populists actively resisted what they called "the money power," by which they meant the increasingly dominant complex of private financial interests associated then as now with Wall Street. We continue to take "the money power" largely for granted today, though its credibility has been shaken in the wake of the financial meltdown of September, 2008. But it was the focus of fierce criticism in the nineteenth century and before. Populists built on earlier precedents in American history—including the experience of home-run colonial currencies, continental money, and the Jeffersonian and Jacksonian opposition to centralized banking—to argue that money and credit ought to be created (loaned into existence) by decentralized public institutions accountable to the public, not by a few private institutions "too big to fail" and accountable mostly to private owners and selective as to whom shall receive credit. Populists further argued that credit should be made available only at a nominal cost–equivalent to what is needed to replace consumed resources—not at the price of usurious interest rates, and that it should be available "bottom-up" to individual citizens at the local level, and not "top-down" by a central bank to commercial banks and large corporations.

What the populists and others pointed out, and what remains true more than ever today, is that the power to create money, charge interest, and control credit is given over to a virtual monopoly exercised by privately owned and largely unaccountable banking and financial interests. Through the mechanism of unnecessary and arbitrary interest rates, wealth is steadily extracted from the general population of borrowers (through mortgages, education loans, credit card debt, consumer loans, taxes to fund government bonds, etc.) and concentrated in the hands of relatively few creditors. The resulting debt trap prevents most people from achieving financial security, leaving them economic dependents, if they are lucky enough to have a job, or otherwise wards of the state (through military service, unemployment insurance, welfare, etc.). The usury-driven industrial revolution over the course of the last two centuries dramatically raised living standards for most of us, to be sure, but only at the cost of resource depletion and ecological overshoot, which are now overtaking us. Populists rightly decried the social injustice of the usurious monetary system. But it turns out, if I am right, that usury—by promoting an unsustainable "growth" economy—perpetuates ecological as well as social injustice. The end of the age of usury promises not only a more just society, but a more sustainable one as well.

I develop Kellogg's scheme in chapter seven as a model financial system for a sustainable society; I offer it as a practical hypothesis, one which is designed, if implemented, to mesh fully with the constraints of sustainable economic life. Consider it a social science thought-experiment: an imaginative construction designed to correct the failings of the current system by providing a way for the public to obtain the credit they need without destroying the planet. This is not a utopian fantasy conceived beyond any possible realization, but as a blueprint of how we might someday better manage our financial affairs, and by extension, our economies and societies. This is not to say its adoption is imminent or even likely today; we are still too wedded to the system which is failing us. But as our current financial orthodoxy loses credibility, we will need to have viable alternatives at hand if we are not to repeat the mistakes of the past, or worse.

NOTES

1. Quote by Niall Ferguson, *The Ascent of Money* (New York: Penguin, 2008), p. 68.

2. Henry Roseveare, *The Financial Revolution 1660–1760* (London: Longman, 1991), p. 41.

3. Ibid., pp. 50, 62.

4. Niall Ferguson, *The Ascent of Money* (New York: Penguin, 2008), p. 99.

5. Two early and widely influential works arguing for limits to growth were *The Limits to Growth*, eds. Donella H. Meadows, et al. (New York: Universe Books, 1972) and *Small is Beautiful*, E. F. Schumacher (New York: Harper & Row, 1973).

6. William R. Catton, Jr., *Overshoot* (Urbana: University of Illinois Press, 1982), p. 158.

7. Ibid., pp. 51–3.

8. Joel E. Cohen, *How Many People Can the Earth Support?* New York: W. W. Norton, 1995), pp. 256–7.

9. A possible scenario linking a credit collapse to a supply-chain and general economic collapse is developed by David Korowicz in *Trade-Off: Financial System Supply-chain Cross-Contagion: A Study in Global Systemic Collapse* (Metis Risk Consulting, www.feasta.org, 30 June 2012, revised).

10. T. R. Malthus, *An Essay on the Principle of Population,* Donald Winch, ed., [1803 edition, showing additions and corrections through the 1826 edition] Cambridge: Cambridge University Press, 1992, p. 25.

11. In this section I largely follow Adam Fergusson, *When Money Dies* (New York: Public Affairs, 2010).

12. Gresham's Law states that people will hoard good money and spend bad money to get rid of it, but the new Rentenmark introduced in 1923, contrary to expectations, found acceptance over the old super inflated mark because the population could not afford to hoard; they were desperate to buy necessities and used the new currency to do so, bringing an end to the hyperinflation. See ibid., pp. 194–5.

Chapter Two

Equal and Unequal Exchanges

The story of credit and usury is the story of the replacement of equal exchanges with unequal ones. Equal exchanges are exchanges of equivalent values, and thereby fully reciprocal. In unequal exchanges values are not equivalent, and therefore not fully reciprocal. Economic exchanges based on barter and commodity monies are generally immediate and transparent, and so are more likely to be equivalent. Credit, by contrast, defers the completion of an exchange, making it less transparent and potentially less than equivalent. Usurious credit in fact institutionalizes unequal exchanges: the debtor by definition is committed under normal circumstances to pay more in the end than he or she borrows at the beginning. The development of credit and usury was a gradual process, with a long and uneven history. An important precondition for the full development of credit and usury was the monetization of key sectors of the economy. As long as money was closely tied to basic production, particularly of agricultural products, its commodity value was more or less evident to all. A consistently reliable coinage (not debased) would have a reasonably consistent value in commodity exchange, reliably purchasing so many bushels of wheat or yards of cloth. In commodity exchanges of this sort, buyers and sellers both could see each side of the exchange and judge accordingly.

During the long agricultural era, from the post-ice age Neolithic to the eighteenth century, land was the principal form of wealth, whether held by the community in some kind of commons, or otherwise controlled either by temples, churches, princes, lords, municipal corporations, or freeholders. Nonetheless, economic activity during this era had a tendency to shift gradually from production for local subsistence to production for exchange in regional, national, and international markets. Goods and services were increasingly monetized, that is, produced not only for direct consumption or barter but for cash. This process reached an early climax in the Europe and the Mediterranean world under the Roman empire, but was set back seriously by the collapse of the western half of the empire in the fifth century. By the early modern period, large sectors of the economy in Italy and northwest Europe were again commercialized and monetized. Picking up where the Roman era left off a thousand years before, wealth began to be detached from land and other more or less illiquid assets, and concentrated in money and related financial instruments (annuities, etc.). The culmination of this process—going beyond Roman precedents—was an unprecedented financial revolution, to be described in the next chapters, which first became apparent in Holland and Britain in the seventeenth century.

Before that financial revolution, late medieval and Renaissance bankers like the Medici and the Fuggers built up reserves mainly in the form of coins issued by sovereign states, as well as uncoined precious metals, jewelry, and similar assets more or less easily convertible into coin. These coins and similar precious objects were forms of commodity money; they represented the distillation of exchange value down to certain convenient items, valuable in themselves, above all precious metals, or specie, especially gold and silver. These were compact, finely divisible, and scarce enough to be in demand, but common enough to be widely used. Commodity money facilitates direct exchange; indeed, insofar as it provides a common medium of exchange, it can be regarded as the perfection of the barter system. Without some kind of commodity (or several of them) acting as a medium (or media) of exchange, even barter would not be practical. Although many economists have written as if money arose out of the demands of barter, a good case can be made that it was the other way around: that it was money which facilitated barter, that is, which made generalized reciprocal exchanges possible.[1] Without some medium of exchange, if my neighbor is willing to give me the bow-and-arrow I want in return for the pair of shoes he or she wants, then I must find some shoes to complete the transaction, not an easy task, and perhaps impossible. A common medium of exchange such as gold or silver, however, if accepted by all parties and more or less accessible to all, conveniently reconciles all such disparate offerings and demands. Gold coins, if perceived to be genuine, will readily be accepted by any seller because he or she will be confident of their intrinsic value, so that they in turn can be expected to be exchanged for something else subsequently desired.

With commodity monies we remain within the circle of equivalent, reciprocal exchanges. I must have the gold coins in my pocket when I go to the market, and be prepared to surrender to the seller an amount of them equivalent to anything I buy. The transaction is immediate, transparent, and complete. Gold and other precious metals are relatively inelastic; their amount can be increased only slowly through the laborious and uncertain process of discovery, mining, and minting. Since their supply at any time is more or less fixed, so is the amount of money they represent. This limits the number of exchanges which can occur. The rate of exchange the amount of money in circulation will allow sets the rate at which the economy as a whole can function, and that rate is a slow one for a monetary system of precious metals.

When vast gold reserves were discovered in the New World in the sixteenth century and imported into Europe, the money supply was dramatically increased, raising the level of economic activity. The new gold was invested in various enterprises, including overseas trade and conquest, creating a commercial boom which resulted in the accumulation of vast capital by European traders. It became apparent to merchants and others in the know that an increase in the money supply would increase the wealth of nations, but no one knew how to increase the money except by finding more gold. Even with the influx from the Americas, however, there still wasn't enough to go around. The world had been brought into a single global trading system for the first time in the sixteenth century, and there simply was too little gold to finance the vast new opportunities which presented themselves. Given the constraints of gold, down to the eighteenth century money (more or less synonymous with gold) almost everywhere was hard to find, and much less in abundance, compared to more recent times.

One way to extend the supply of money, at least temporarily, is through credit. We know that credit is an old as commodity money, and that since the earliest times it has been used to ameliorate the scarcity of even the most reliable forms of commodity money. A form of credit was already practiced at the very beginning of recorded history, in the ancient Sumerian cities, where large temple complexes calculated accounts of debts on cuneiform tablets, thousands of which have survived.[2] The unit of reckoning was no abstract token, however, but the silver shekel, the equivalent of a bushel of barley.[3] The shekel—not a coin but a weight of silver—was a form of commodity money. Debts, though calculated in shekels, could be settled by any number of valuable commodities, from grain to livestock to precious stones. Credit was extended as a token of existing or reliably anticipated value, something that can be easily and tangibly defined, e.g., next year's crop, goods received from a trading expedition, etc. This development of credit seems to have been a function of the unique position of the Mesopotamian region. As Michael Hudson explains, that region ". . . needed to create an export surplus to exchange for the foreign metals, stone and other raw materials not found in its own river-deposited soils. It also needed to keep families on the land self-sustaining to ensure a supply of fighters in the almost constant warfare of the epoch."[4] The temple complexes achieved these goals by advancing assets to merchants and farmers from the surpluses they were able to accumulate from their lands and workshops. As Hudson points out, this meant that the central authority (the temple) was the creditor for the society, in contrast to the situation today where the central authority (the government) is the debtor, not the creditor, of society.

It would be a mistake, however, to see ancient Mesopotamia as a full-blown credit economy. Hudson makes the point:

> Credit only seems to have served as a source of spending for merchants or consumers vis-à-vis their immediate suppliers, not involving bankers pyramiding of IOUs. The term 'credit' therefore should be avoided in the sense used by economists today. Money-loans were limited to advances from existing hoards, often to merchants to obtain goods to trade, as well as by merchants to their own customers. Such loans also included the advance of land to cultivators, and the sub-contracting of palace or temple workshops and other enterprises to private or semi-private operators. These activities were more in the character of rental agreements than loans . . . There was no 'credit multiplier' in which spending or lending power based on one person's IOU is used as an asset by his (or her) creditor."[5]

In other words, the key mechanisms for multiplying this simple indebtedness familiar to us today—such as fractional reserve banking, credit markets, etc.—were unknown in ancient times.

Ancient types of credit in fact operated within the circle of reciprocity, and it would be misleading to give credit the fundamental role in earlier societies that it has achieved only recently.[6] I define reciprocity broadly to include not just direct and immediate exchanges, but short-term or seasonal re-balancing of accounts. The assumption remained that debts and payments would and should even out at a near fixed date: when the crops were in, or when the trading caravans or merchant ships returned. Interest was commonly charged, insofar as it could be justified by such reasonable risks and expenses as might be involved. Of course, the use of credit was liable to abuse, and interest charges could become extortionary; indeed, usurious rates were widespread. But they did not yet dominate the local exchanges of the subsistence economies of the day, let alone transform them. Even so, although early credit remained within the circle of commodity exchange, it nonetheless opened the door to unequal exchanges important enough to spark significant social struggle. Much of the social tension in ancient societies down to the Greeks and Romans revolved around oppressive indebtedness, particularly of otherwise "free" landowners indebted to merchants or other wealthy creditors.

Rather than permitting excessive indebtedness to go indefinitely unchecked and wreck economic life, however, most ancient societies invoked some sort of periodic cancellation of debts, perhaps the best known being the "law of jubilee" from the Old Testament, which called for the cancellation of debts every seven years. In a kind of religious reset of the economy, the Babylonians may have abolished some debts every New Year, and it was common for new rulers to proclaim a cancellation of debts when they ascended the throne. Debt thus was not allowed to stray too far from its transparent commodity moorings. This stands in stark contrast to modern societies where perpetual indebtedness is virtually unchallenged and the value of money is uncertain over time, and constantly in flux. Cancellation of debts, in whole or part, figured prominently in attempts to resolve the class struggles in ancient Greek city states and in Rome, though by the late Roman empire debt issues had become chronic and insoluble. Partly in reaction to this, usury was finally declared illegal by the Church, after which it remained suppressed for more than a millennium. Unending usurious debt, in other words, was not (as it is in the modern world) accepted as a fact of life. Today the idea of a cancellation of debts is a kind of shocking secular heresy, presented, if discussed at all, as an almost unthinkable catastrophe.

The true revolution of modernity, in the view of this work, was a financial revolution, one which gave us our modern credit system. Its basis was the invention of a new monetary system in which money, though still tied to precious metals for a long time, was made much more plentiful through leveraging loans and legalizing usurious credit. The development of new forms of credit on a large scale amounted to the invention of a new form of money. This new money was slowly but steadily divorced from any kind of commodity status, and increasingly transformed into an ever-amplified series of open-ended claims against future resources. The multiplication of these claims beyond any reasonable plausibility has created the many trillions of dollars of debt on the books today—a total far beyond any likely ability to be redeemed. The last step in the disengagement of credit money from any commodity was the suspension of international gold payments by the United States government in 1971. Since then, the dollar and all major world currencies have been pure fiat money—that is, money legally proclaimed as such with only the backing of the credit and police power of the state.

While the other ingredients of the industrial revolution might have been necessary conditions for its realization, it was only the explosion of credit which allowed those ingredients to be fully exploited for the first time. Unfortunately, this was done in such a way as to concentrate wealth in the hands of a few, and to impose burdens of usurious interest payments on debtors in specific, and on society as a whole. It didn't have to be this way. Credit might have been made available without excessive interest rates attached, as we shall see, and various proposals were made in the seventeenth century and since to that end, but it was not to be. Instead, a system of credit was invented, to be described more fully in subsequent chapters, by which private interests were able to appropriate what used to be the right of the sovereign to issue money, and to use that right as the basis for inflating the money supply, many times over, by lending it out at high rates of interest.

But many obstacles had to be overcome first. Lending at more than a rate of interest equivalent to the replacement of the loan had long been condemned as usury by the church, effectively discouraging people with money to lend. Jews, the only significant group in Europe outside the church in the Middle Ages, were allowed to lend at interest to gentiles, though not to one another, but their resources were too limited to spark a wholesale economic transformation. Debts were widely incurred, of course, but for most ordinary people debts were commonly without usurious interest (which was prohibited) and based rather on a personal, relatively short-term basis, usually as an advance against future production, e.g., in the expectation of a crop to be harvested or a product to be made. Most of the economy functioned not on borrowed money, as it does today, but on direct exchanges on a local subsistence level (local production of food and commodities cleared through local markets); business was done mostly through fully reciprocal exchanges, even where credit was involved. Credit in such traditional exchanges was a supplement to, but not a replacement for, commodity money.

There were important exceptions to this dominant localism, of course, including trade in some textiles, luxury goods, and some basic commodities, all of which required a greater role for credit; much of this was significant long-term trade (luxury goods from the East through Venice and other Italian cities, grain from Poland to Western Europe, etc.), but even this largely supplemented and did not yet replace the subsistence economy. As long as land remained the basis of wealth, and financial transactions could be cleared only on the basis of commodity monies, the bulk of production was tied to the seasons, the weather, and the vagaries of agriculture in one's neighborhood, that is, to a regime of renewable more or less steady-state production, with *no expectation* of any steady increase in production, or growth. Nonagricultural production, vital as it was, remained limited by the constraints on land and agriculture, and since agricultural credit could be no more productive than next year's crop, and since other resources, such as metals, etc., could be obtained only by using limited renewable energy, there was no way to facilitate steady increases in production, even in non-agricultural sectors, as subsequently became common. Usury in this context was a straightforward abuse of the system, the transgression by one or another unscrupulous lender; it was not a systematic feature of the monetary system, as it became after the financial revolution.

In spite of these monetary limitations, including reliance on scarce precious metals for money, with the increase in trade in Europe following the Crusades, and especially after the establishment of new commercial contacts in Asia and the Americas, more and more goods and services were monetized, that is, available for purchase in markets in exchange for cash, while credit gradually expanded. Yet local exchanges in kind and cooperative sharing of labor and resources outside the cash-nexus long persisted in most sectors, even as they slowly and steadily contracted. From the late Middle Ages, first in Italy, and then in parts of France, the German principalities, the Low Countries, the Baltic region, and England, commercial centers developed, particularly in the free cities and small states, which became the focal points of the new trading networks. A tipping point, as we shall see, was reached by the seventeenth century in Holland, and soon after in important centers throughout northwestern Europe, including England, when key sectors of the economy, including land itself, became monetized. Instead of remaining an inalienable possession held in feudal tenure by lords, secular and religious, who were as much tied to their estates as were their peasants, land gradually came to be redefined in terms of fee simple ownership, that is, something with a price, alienable, more easily bought and sold in a real estate market, a market like any other monetized market. The monetization of land was a slow process which came to include not only private estates and freeholds but also the commons. In a series of steps—the enclosures, from the sixteenth to the nineteenth centuries—much of the previous commons in a number of European countries was brought into the monetized sphere. This large-scale monetization was the prelude, as we shall see, to the financial revolution.

The initial result was a transformation of agriculture, particularly in Britain, an important but not yet decisive step towards the industrial revolution. In the words of economic historian Pierre Vilar,

> The agrarian structure of England had already begun [in the early modern era] to be disturbed by the impact of a monetary economy. The move to enclosures had begun in the 16th century, and more and more small peasant plots and communal lands were engulfed by great private estates. This made way for a change in the nature of agriculture, and an escape from a small-scale subsistence economy. In England the commercialization of agricultural products had been going on since the Middle Ages. These profound changes in the economy and society of England produced two political revolutions: the Cromwellian revolution and the 'Glorious Revolution' of 1688. . . . there is no doubt that by the end of the century, the views and interests of the 'moneyed men' of England, who had at first been despised, now held sway, even in affairs of state, and prevailed over those of the landed interests.[7]

These new 'monied men' were traders, brokers, and speculators who made money not by producing anything but by exploiting financial opportunities in the new markets. Once the prohibitions against usury were broken down in the wake of the Reformation, as we shall see, what money was available could be lent out at a profit, and so could be used to reproduce itself—that is, it could now be expected to increase as repayments exceeded the original principal lent out—vastly enhancing its value and power. As a result, money was steadily transformed from a fixed hard currency in hand into a contract, a future promise of payment compounding the original investment. Usury not only proceeded in parallel with monetization; it magnified and transformed it. The more money there was, especially after the gold influx from America, the more easily and profitably it could be lent, and the more convenient and even necessary it became to concentrate wealth in money, other than in more fixed, less fungible assets, especially land. The power of these 'moneyed men' expanded accordingly, as money and credit played an ever larger role in economic life. Money and credit—which in the preindustrial era, it cannot be overemphasized, were constrained by the limits of agricultural production and the relative scarcity of precious metals—were not only liberated but put in command of the economy. This novel expansion of money and especially credit in early modern Europe was stimulated initially by the rise of trade and commerce; but, once established, the new forms of money and credit in a feedback effect dramatically stimulated trade and commerce, and—given the startling financial innovations to be discussed in chapters three and four— eventually prompted the industrial revolution itself, and the birth of the modern world as we know it.

The new monetary order of credit underlying modernity is not to be confused with or simply numbered among the technical material innovations we normally associate with the industrial revolution and the rise of the "growth" economy. Rather it preceded and enabled them. Unlike the steam engine or railroad or telegraph or any other mechanical innovation, credit is not a material thing; it is rather a peculiar attitude towards material things institutionalized into a contract, an agreement to use some of those things in new ways. An agreement to use credit is what philosophers call a performative act; a good example would be getting married. When the officiating authority at a wedding says "I pronounce you man and wife," he or she invokes and applies a binding public contract governing certain aspects of future human behavior for the subjects in question, and it is exactly the same with taking out a loan. Signing the loan papers at the bank is as much a binding public contract as getting married, as much a ritual, and is in fact harder to get out of! Credit introduced a new way of thinking, its principal feature being the ability to facilitate and appropriate *future* production. Reciprocity and transparency were replaced by growth and uncertainty.

Future uses, potentially very advantageous ones, are brought into current calculations by monetizing future values through debt. Credit, when combined with usurious rates of interest, is an obligation not only for future production, but for *increased* future production to cover the usurious interest. In antiquity credit was available, often at usurious rates, but it was not essential to the economy and it did not lead to economic growth. It was only in the decades around 1700, beginning in Britain, that usurious credit, for the first time, was put at the center of economic life and became the engine of growth. It is this additional obligation of usury, I suggest, which has been the main engine and driving force of modern economic development. As we shall see in more detail, credit was rapidly made much more widely available by a private banking system which, after the Bank of England was established in 1694, could make loans backed by government resources, including tax revenues. A privatized financial system was granted not only a public monopoly to issue money as debt, but it was allowed to charge usurious rates for providing this service. The rub was that the availability of this new credit, now conditional on usurious interest rates, guaranteed an unprecedented debt burden for many borrowers, and unearned profits for a relatively few creditors. Inequality was institutionalized.

Lenders of money from the beginning of time have customarily demanded some kind of return for their risk, which is how we often regard interest on loans. How much interest to charge has long been a vexed and thorny issue. Immoderate rates of interest, however defined, were widely condemned as usurious, not only by the Catholic Church but in Muslem countries as well. That the abolition of usury by the Council of Nicaea in the fourth century seems to have been imposed without serious economic dislocation is evidence that the Roman economy as a whole did not run on usurious credit. The medieval Catholic Church by and large kept the lid on usury in the West. As financial historian Niall Ferguson reminds us, "Usurers, people who lent money at interest, had been excommunicated by the Third Lateran Council in 1179. Even arguing that usury was not a sin had been condemned as heresy by the Council of Vienna in 1311-12."[8] Even the Medici banks did not charge interest, though they arranged some compensation, or *discrezione*, to their depositors.[9] But with the rise of commerce in the later Middle Ages, as we've seen, attitudes began to change. The Reformation, Counter-Reformation, and subsequent religious wars called into question established values and opened the way for the emergence of commercial and pecuniary attitudes in their own right, not as subservient to some other belief system. The Protestant Reformation, by splitting religious authority into competing sects, undermined the once unitary power of the Catholic Church to enforce its morality, including its prohibition of usurious interest on loans. The cat was out of the bag.

The legitimization of usury—permanently in England from 1571,[10] with some limits remaining on very high rates—was to prove decisive for Western and eventually world history. Martin Luther vacillated on the question of usury, resisting it as an evil; yet he increasingly accommodated some degree of interest on loans to satisfy the secular commercial and political powers who supported his movement.[11] On the conceptual level, the ice was finally broken by John Calvin. The Catholic prohibition had been based on a Biblical passage, Deuteronomy 23, verses 19-20, which in the King James version reads: "Thou shalt not lend upon usury to thy brother; usury of money, usury of victuals, usury of any thing that is lent upon usury. Unto a stranger thou

mayest lend upon usury; but unto thy brother thou shalt not lend upon usury . . ." If usury was forbidden within the brotherhood of the Jewish community, should it not be forbidden with the brotherhood of the Christian community, as the Catholic church argued? Calvin's shifty answer was that

> usury is not now unlawful, except insofar as it contravenes equity and brother-
> ly union. Let each one, then, place himself before God's judgment seat, and
> not do to his neighbor what he would not have done to himself, from whence a
> sure and infallible decision may be come to. To exercise the trade of usury . . .
> is much less tolerable among the children of God; but in what cases, and how
> far it may be lawful to receive usury upon loans, the law of equity will better
> prescribe than any lengthened discussions. [12]

If lenders and borrowers are willing to lend and borrow on usurious terms, in
other words, then the way is open for them to do so.

The importance of the spirit of Protestantism to the birth of capitalism,
and therefore the industrial revolution and modernity, was a point made long
ago by Max Weber in his influential work, *The Protestant Ethic and the
Spirit of Capitalism*. It seems that commercial values—buying and selling to
make money, or capitalism—for the first time in history in the wake of the
Reformation stood forth independently of other values on a cultural scale
more or less as Weber argued. Indeed, just this may be taken as a sign of the
maturity the commercial revolution finally achieved in this era. The commercial revolution—the liberation of trade and credit from most religious and
political constraints—was a capitalist revolution, to be sure, but not yet an
industrial one. Capitalism is the more or less unrestricted pursuit of wealth
through investment. Just as Weber argued that Protestantism, especially Cal-
vinism, was the incubator of capitalism as an independent cultural phenomenon, I propose in turn that capitalism—the new, monetized commercial economy—was the incubator of the larger usurious credit economy, [13] and that in
due course that usurious credit economy was the incubator of what has become an all-encompassing industrial revolution. Weber is careful to point out
that the spirit of capitalism, once born out of the ethic of Protestantism, took
on a life of its own. Capitalism is not to be identified with Protestantism; it
may more fruitfully be considered one of its children. And similarly, the
credit economy can be understood as a child of capitalism, and finally usury
can be seen as a child of the credit economy, no doubt a wayward child but a
child nonetheless—comprising a family tree, if you will, of four generations.
Weber focused on the first two generations. I endeavor in what follows to
trace the course of the two generations subsequent to these: to show how the
credit economy gave birth to usury, which in turn gave birth to the industrial
revolution and the modern world of endless growth.

The modern credit economy is above all a *usurious* credit economy. This
author, at least, does not believe in historical inevitability; things could have

been otherwise. But an opportunity was seized, by the 'monied men' in London at the turn of the seventeenth century to attach usurious rates to credit and put them at the center of a national economy. Credit since has been made widely available in modern times for many purposes, as never before, but as a rule only on condition of a profit through excessive interest charges made by creditors, charges which generally exceed the creditor's expenses, trouble, and risk. This profit is not only expected, but legally guaranteed to the utmost extent possible under the contract of the loan, with such contracts enforced by the power of the state. Credit-for-profit of this sort is *not* essential to capitalism, if by capitalism we mean simply the intentional accumulation of capital, that is, money or resources reserved not for consumption but to create more resources. One can accumulate capital in a variety of ways without recourse to credit—for instance, by arbitrage (finding markets where one can buy low and sell high), by direct investment in productive enterprises (owning a business or rental property), by war, and even by criminal activity (piracy, slave trade, extortion, etc.). The idea of credit-for-profit, or usury, is only one technique for accumulating capital, but it is a particularly potent one. Without it, the modern world as we know it would not exist. This is why it is vital to understand how the usurious credit economy was born from other, earlier forms of commerce and capitalism.

The term usury generally refers, as I am using it, to excessive or unearned interest on loans, which amounts to a kind of arbitrary tax or tribute on the borrower. There can be credit without usury or any interest at all, we should not forget, insofar as assets may be borrowed or lent with no expectation of gain, but simply on the basis of redemption at face value; here, as perhaps in a family loan, no profit need be made or expected. There can also be credit with interest which is not usurious, as when the interest goes to cover the unavoidable costs and risks associated with a loan. The general benchmark for this, as I shall argue later, is the replenishment value of the original loan in repayment. It is only when credit is used to elicit some *greater* return for the lender beyond legitimate expenses and risks, that is, the actual costs of replacing materials and resources at the time of repayment, that credit turns into usury, into an unequal exchange.

Although it is important to distinguish credit from interest, and interest from usury, virtually all available credit in modern economies has been usurious. Exactly when a rate of interest becomes usurious has been a contentious issue historically, and we shall clarify it further in more detail in chapter six as we peel away one layer of misunderstanding after another. Here we need only point out that usury upsets the traditional principle of reciprocity; it not only insists on getting back from the transaction more than it puts in, but it seeks to minimize if not eliminate risk. One classic historian of money and finance, R. H. Tawney, writing of the medieval anti-usury tradition, puts it nicely:

> What remained to the end unlawful [in that tradition] was that which appears
> in modern economic textbooks as 'pure interest'—interest as a fixed payment
> stipulated in advance for a loan of money or wares without risk to the lend-
> er. . . . The essence of usury was that it was certain, and that, whether the
> borrower gained or lost, the usurer took his pound of flesh. [14]

The lender, in this context, in return for advancing money to the borrower, hopes to profit from the borrower's productive assets—skills, labor power, prospects of advancement, property, etc.,—with the borrower's collateral put up as insurance to the lender in case of default. We do not normally think of the lender as invoking and appropriating the borrower's expanded productive power, but that is a clear premise of the transaction. It is the borrower's assets which are being utilized, through usury, first of all to the benefit of the creditor, and only secondarily to the benefit of the lender, after the creditor is satisfied. I may borrow money for consumption, say when I take out a car loan. But insofar as a borrower can use the money borrowed not for consumption but for some investment, he or she is also using someone else's assets (the lender's money) to magnify his or her gain. This is what is conventionally understood as leveraging. The leverage of the debtor lies in his or her use of the assets of the creditor—the money lent—to produce extra wealth sufficient to make a profit while paying off the creditor.

Usury and leverage are two sides of the same coin. Usury, as the term is generally used, puts the focus on the lender, who has the power of the state to enforce contracts as a guarantee of repayment. Leverage puts the focus on the borrower, who hopes to gain but who does not have the protections afforded the lender. Both seek to accumulate profit, or capital. It is convenient to use the term usury to cover both situations. Notice the underlying presumption of growth—or the prospect thereof—without which usury makes no sense. *Usury demands and requires economic growth.* As long as there are resources available to exploit the economy can grow and usurious debts can be discharged. But insofar as resources become scarce relative to demand, then growth becomes difficult if not impossible, and usurious debts cannot be paid. Hence the boom and bust cycle characteristic of usurious economies. What is new here is that the entire industrial period of modernity appears increasingly as a gigantic boom, one which portends a gigantic bust.

Let me end this chapter with two general observations. First, the importance of usurious credit in establishing unequal exchanges suggests an alternative explanatory narrative of social injustice. The traditional social critique of modern economic and social relations is associated with left-wing politics in general, and with Marxism in particular. Its focus is on the exploitation of labor by capital, with the capitalist understood to be short-changing the workers by unfairly appropriating a share of their labor-value. This takes the form of the commodification of labor, according to the Marxists, whereby labor is bought and sold in the marketplace like any other good or service. Since the price of commodified labor depends on factors other than the value labor brings to the product—e.g., supply and demand, etc.—the capitalist is able to appropriate that extra value whenever the price of labor is less, as it normally is, than the price of the products of labor. As Marx put it in *Wage Labour and Capital*: "The worker receives means of subsistence in exchange for his labour power, but the capitalist receives in exchange for his means of subsistence labour, the productive activity of the worker, the creative power whereby the worker not only replaces what he consumes but *gives to the accumulated labour a greater value than it previously possessed*." (emphasis by Marx)[15]

What is far less clear in Marx, however, is how this state of affairs came to pass to begin with. In *Capital*, he raises the question:

> One thing however is clear—Nature does not produce on the one side owners of money and commodities, and on the other men possessing nothing but their own labour-power. This relation has no natural basis, neither is its social basis one that is common to all historical periods. It is clearly the result of a past historical development, the product of many economic revolutions, of the extinction of a whole series of forms of social production.[16]

If our analysis of money and credit is correct, it is the prior compulsion to meet the demands of usurious credit which was (and still is) fundamental in motivating capitalists to lower costs, including labor costs—something about which Marx has very little to say. The commodification of labor indeed was no accident, but the result of a long series of deliberate policies aimed at breaking down the guild system and other institutions, such as the traditional commons, which were designed to retain full value for producers. These policies include the enclosure movement, the slave trade, the 'putting out system,' cottage industry, and ultimately the wage labor and factory system itself. Without the financial revolution—to be discussed in the following chapters—there arguably would have been little incentive or opportunity to dismantle the feudal structures protecting producers, and the hyper-capitalism of the modern era might never have developed.

The appreciation of the central role of finance in modern social and economic history is not to be found the socialist left, but in the populist tradition.[17] In that tradition the basic conflict is not between capital and labor but between creditors and debtors. "Conflict between creditors and debtors," writes Philip Coggan,

> is almost as old as money itself. John Taylor, an early nineteenth-century American thinker, said that the banking industry 'divides the nations into two groups, creditors and debtors and fills each with malignity towards the other.' One can see all of economic history through this prism—a battle between

those who lend money and those who borrow it. The former want to be paid
back with interest in sound money; in times of crisis, the debtors cannot afford
to do so.[18]

The driving mechanism of exploitation, in this view, is the extraction of
interest, not the extraction of surplus labor value. The latter indeed takes
place, and has taken place in a variety of forms since the beginning of
history, but it is only with the imposition of usurious interest rates that the
exploitation of labor—and natural resources—becomes ruthlessly accelerat-
ed to meet the demands of endless growth.

The classic Marxian worker is forced into a subsistence existence; because of that, he or she, deprived of capital resources and dependent on
wage-labor, doesn't have the minimal surplus necessary to carry a debt. Only
with twentieth century consumerism were traditional workers able to earn
enough to go into debt. Today debtors comprise a much larger group than
laborers; many debtors have never been laborers at all, especially not Marx-
ian-type wage-laborers. The ranks of debtors have always been extremely
varied, from monarchs and aristocrats, to merchants, corporations, entrepreneurs, small business people, farmers, manufacturers, and investors leveraging
borrowed money, among others. The real dynamic of modern economics lies
in the interplay of these diverse debtors and their creditors. The class warfare
of debtors and creditors, now as in ancient times, is a better measure of social
conflict than that between labor and capital.

Finally, if some philosophical speculation may be permitted, it is worth
noting that the invention of modern credit involved, among other things, the
identification of time with money, something not seen earlier. Once this
identification became institutionalized, once everyday life came to be conditioned more or less by the demands of credit, time itself came to be redefined. In the commodity based monetary systems of the past, where credit
was a secondary not a primary monetary phenomenon, time had little compulsion attached to it. Tomorrow was not expected to be significantly different from today, and the round of life replicated rather than transcended itself.
But after the financial revolution of the seventeenth and eighteenth centuries,
debtors found themselves compelled to make the future different from the
past. And as credit became central to the economy and to society, society as a
whole found itself similarly compelled. The necessity to continually increase
production entailed both the promise of an earthly utopia as well as new
levels of anxiety and stress now inseparable from the efforts required to
increase production. It is perhaps no accident that the standardization of time
in Newtonian physics corresponded roughly with the institutionalization of
credit in Britain.

On a social level, this standardization of time came to be embodied, for
instance, in the precise railway schedules established in the nineteenth centu-

ry, where local time was abolished in favor of a uniform national, indeed global system of time zones, where departures and arrivals were calculated to the minute. In addition, the incorporation of usurious rates of interest into the credit system had the effect of accelerating the process of time: the more effort required to keep up with exponential growth, the more quickly time seemed to pass. The logical conclusion of this process is captured in a recent science fiction film, *In Time*, where time is literally monetized.[19] Human beings stop aging at 25 years of age, and are programmed to live only one more year unless they can accumulate additional units of time, which function as the currency of society. With ever additional units of time, it is possible to achieve effective immortality. The rich are able to do this by depriving the bulk of society of the time they need to live by lending out to them time as money at usurious rates of interest. As a result, they are in a position to accumulate the time they need to survive, while debtors eventually run out of time and die. In this dystopian nightmare parable of greed and finance, the ultimate corruption of the usurious credit system is dramatically displayed.

NOTES

1. See David Graeber, *Debt: The First 5,000 Years* (Brooklyn: Melville House, 2011), pp. 21–41.

2. See Michael Hudson, "Reconstructing the Origins of Interest-Bearing Debt and the Logic of Clean Slates," in *Debt and Economic Revival in the Ancient Near East* (Bethesda: CDL Press, 2002), pp. 7–58.

3. Ibid., p. 23.

4. Ibid., p. 21.

5. Ibid., p. 49.

6. David Graeber (see note 1 above) is one author who recognizes an important role for credit far back into history, but it seems, as Hudson makes clear (note 2 above), that credit remained well within the limits of reciprocal exchanges characteristic of traditional societies until it was institutionalized on the basis of central banking, government debt, and credit markets in the eighteenth century, as we discuss in chapters 3 and 4 of this work.

7. Pierre Vilar, *A History of Gold and Money: 1450-1920*, Judith White, trans. (New York: Verso, 1976), pp. 212–3.

8. Niall Ferguson, *The Ascent of Money* (New York: Penguin Press, 2008), p. 35.

9. Ibid., p. 44.

10. A limit of 10 percent, later 6 percent, was imposed on interest, though the government was exempt. See P. G. M. Dickson, *The Financial Revolution* (London: Macmillan, 1967, p. 41.

11. See Benjamin Nelson, *The Idea of Usury: From Tribal Brotherhood to Universal Otherhood*, 2nd ed. (Chicago: University of Chicago Press, 1969), pp. 29–72.

12. Quoted in Ibid., p. 79.

13. Indeed Benjamin Nelson in a footnote in his *The Idea of Usury* (note 11 above) ties in Max Weber's thesis of the relationship between Protestantism and capitalism to usury even more closely: "Had Weber had the opportunity to pursue the insights of his last lectures, he might well have hit upon the fact that Calvin's view of usury was one of the first monuments of the Universal Otherhood, whose characteristics he had so well envisaged. For reasons too complex to recall here, it was not until the end of his life that he detected the fruitfulness of taking the usury question as a point of departure for the history of the capitalist spirit." (p, 74).

14. R. H. Tawney, *Religion and the Rise of Capitalism: A Historical Study* (London: John Murray, 1926

15. Karl Marx, *Wage Labour and Capital* in *The Marx-Engels Reader*, Robert C. Tucker, ed. (New York: W. W. Norton, 1972), p. 178.

16. Karl Marx, *Capital*, vol. 1 (New York: International Publishers, 1967), p. 169.

17. See my earlier work: *Fixing the System* (New York: Continuum Books, 2008).

18. Philip Coggan, *Paper Promises: Debt, Money, and the New World Order* (New York: Public Affairs, 2012), p. 6.

19. *In Time*, Andrew Nichol, Director (Regency Enterprises: 2011); seehttp://en.wikipedia.org/wiki/In_Time.

Chapter Three

The Commercial Revolution

The story I wish to tell—the sequence of commercial, financial, and industrial revolutions—goes back to the decentralized subsistence economy which emerged from the collapse of the Roman empire in Europe. It was out of that subsistence economy that the first of our revolutions, the commercial revolution, gradually took shape over many centuries. In the depths of the so-called dark ages—the five hundred years from the sixth to the eleventh centuries—long-distance trade was sketchy at best. Local production for local needs, mostly exchanges in kind with little in the way of production for trade, became the norm. Uniform Roman gold coins were gradually replaced by a variety of regionally minted silver coins, used almost exclusively in local (weekly) markets for small purchases. In Capetian France alone, master-historian Henri Pirenne tells us, "300 vassals had appropriated the right of coinage."[1] Credit also continued, but almost entirely on a personal and seasonal basis for consumption purposes; the church effectively banned usury. Cities were miniscule by modern (or ancient) standards. Although money never ceased circulating, its quantity was vastly diminished. The feudal system was slowly built upon this surviving rural base; it gradually developed and modified this subsistence economy, but never transcended it. Long-distance trade gradually improved and cities began to grow, but local production for local consumption remained the rule, even in the high Middle Ages in the thirteenth and fourteenth centuries up to the Black Death—a period when the feudal system achieved a kind of perfection much admired by some medieval historians.

Henri Pirenne's description of the early medieval era has been little improved upon:

It is quite plain, from such evidence as we possess, that from the end of the eighth century Western Europe had sunk back into a purely agricultural state. Land was the sole source of subsistence and the sole condition of wealth. All classes of the population, from the Emperor, who had no other revenues than those derived from his landed property, down to the humblest serf, lived directly or indirectly on the products of the soil, whether they raised them by their labour, or confined themselves to collecting and consuming them. Movable wealth no longer played any part in economic life. All social existence was founded on property or on the possession of land. Hence it was impossible for the state to keep up a military system and an administration which were not based on it. The army was now recruited only from among the holders of fiefs and the officials from among the great landowners. In these circumstances, it became impossible to safeguard the sovereignty of the head of the State. If it existed in principle, it disappeared in practice. The feudal system simply represents the disintegration of public authority in the hands of its agents, who, by reason of the very fact that each one of them held a portion of the soil, had become independent and considered the authority with which they were invested as part of their patrimony. In fact, the appearance of feudalism in Western Europe in the course of the ninth century was nothing but the repercussion in the political sphere of the return of society to a purely rural civilization. [2]

Although trade, commerce, and urban life began to revive in the twelfth century, stimulated during the era of the first Crusades by renewed contact with the Muslim world and the East, the decentralized rural feudal economy continued to be dominant. Cities were small and the bulk of the population lived in the countryside where most exchanges were made in kind, not in cash. No medieval manor was entirely isolated and wholly self-sufficient, but most were remarkably so. The transition from a mainly in-kind economy to a mainly cash economy occurred, at least in England, in the fourteenth century after the Black Death. The acute labor shortage which followed in its wake allowed many peasants the bargaining power they needed to liberate themselves from serfdom and enter the rural wage labor market. [3] At the same time, the new wealth now concentrated in the small but growing cities attracted the attention of princes seeking to recentralize authority. Princely incomes were mostly payments in kind from their estates, with too little cash (coin in those days) available to fund an effective armed force, as Pirenne notes. As a result monarchs resorted to loans, forced or otherwise, from the only people who had money: the merchants of the cities, and later, the urban money-changers who evolved into the first bankers. The merchants and bankers could hardly refuse such patrons. So the monarchs went into debt to merchant-bankers, the most prominent being from the Italian cities. It was a tricky business, marked by numerous defaults. One of the most spectacular was the default of Edward III of England in 1339. His default, which bankrupted his creditors, the Florentine bankers Bardi and Peruzzi among others, might be counted as the first modern financial crash.

Though it was a local, not a systemic failure (there being no systemic credit system, as we know it today), defaults such as Edward III's became increasingly typical of monarchs in the late medieval and early modern eras. In their desperation for cash to fund the endless cycle in warfare in which they were trapped, princes resorted to a series of self-defeating expedients, including debasement of coinage, sale of offices, sale or mortgage of crown lands, tax farming, and forced loans. Given the continued strong feudal principles of reciprocity and local rights, and the relative scarcity of money, princes were almost powerless to impose taxes as we know them. Debasement and the importation of precious metals from America, which inflated the money supply, forced monarchs to borrow ever more while incomes from traditional sources lagged behind. Only with the *taille* in France in 1438 did a monarch succeeded in establishing a permanent tax, but it long remained an exception, not the rule.

There was for princes no alternative to borrowing money. As a result of repeated defaults, especially in Spain and the German states, and of desperate measures to raise money elsewhere (such as Henry VIII's dissolution of the monasteries in England from 1536), European monarchs found themselves ever weaker.[4] The Spanish crown suspended payments on its debts, in part or in whole, in 1557, 1560, 1575, 1596, 1607, 1627, 1647, 1651, and 1662.[5] Even Queen Elizabeth of England, famous for never defaulting, could not stem the financial tide against her. As one financial historian reports,

> Elizabeth's ordinary revenue from Crown lands, Customs, etc., at her accession was £200,000. By her death it has risen to £300,000. From taxation she was able to raise on an average about £50,000 a year at the beginning of her reign and £80,000 at the end. In other words her revenue was increasing less rapidly than prices were rising, while the revenue itself in the first place was revenue adequate for the expenses of government at the price-level of Henry VIII's time rather than that of the latter half of the century.[6]

The financial calamities of the English monarchs led eventually to the Civil War of the seventeenth century and finally, as we shall see, to the financial revolution which found its political expression in England in the aftermath of the Glorious Revolution of 1688. This particular monarchy was saved, but at the price of surrendering *de facto* sovereignty to a financial oligarchy.

The medieval financial system—personalized, reciprocal, decentralized, non-usurious, and commodified (silver and later gold coin)—persisted through the seventeenth century and much later in many places. The princes of the day were frustrated by it. As individual contracts, royal debts were on the person of the reigning monarch, and not on his or her heirs, unless they were also personally contracted. Royal debts were not obligations of what we today would call the state, but of private individuals. Princes had to enter the narrow credit markets of the day like anyone else, as debtors, not creditors, in spite of their vast estates and other resources, which unfortunately for them could not produce enough income to fund their wars and other needs. There were no open financial markets to trade royal notes, or other similar financial instruments. This was, as we might say today, a structural problem. In the meantime, a new and highly productive form of money had been invented by the merchants centered in cities, who were beginning to dominate increasingly powerful commercial networks, but the monarchs were not part of it.

One of the advantages of the cities was their corporate rather than personal organization. As corporations, cities were perpetual entities, freed of the obligations attendant upon the disposal of estates at death. They were thereby able, unlike monarchs and other individuals, to transform personal ground rents or other assets into local public debt. As another financial historian, Robert E. Wright, notes, "By the sixteenth century, Low Country local governments in cities like Leiden, Haarlem, and Amsterdam, as well as the Dutch provincial government, were also able to borrow long-term by mortgaging taxes."[7] Burghers (led by merchants) were generally members of municipal corporations which shared risk. Cities sold annuities, for instance, from an early date, based on their local tax revenue and other municipal income, creating concentrations of capital for investment available to merchants but not to monarchs. Annuities were not included under the ban on usury since they could not be repurchased, though they could be sold to third parties. Cities also resorted to forced loans from their citizens, but their corporate nature as perpetually existing bodies allowed them options on such loans unavailable to princes. Florence, for example, transformed its forced loans into negotiable debt instruments with interest (usury also did not apply to forced loans); these could be bought and sold. Historian Niall Ferguson makes the point: "In effect, then, Florence turned its citizens into its biggest investors. By the early fourteenth century, two thirds of households had contributed in this way to financing the public debt, though the bulk of subscriptions were accounted for by a few thousand wealthy individuals."[8]

This concentration of capital in cities, in part through annuities and public debt, is summarized by yet another financial historian, Richard Ehrenberg:

> The rentier, towards the end of the Middle Ages, was a not infrequent phenomenon in the cities. Besides the corporations and foundations there were everywhere widows and orphans whose incomes consisted solely of annuities. It seems that in many of the cities of the Netherlands, as early as the fourteenth century, the manual workers (*Ambachts-Luyde*) nicknamed the rentiers as a class apart, *Ledichganghers* or 'the idlers.' The chief families, apart from trade, lived on annuities. We know that the cities carried on a kind of banking business for this purpose, and we can easily see how they in this way collected

capital, not only their own citizens, but also from those of neighboring and friendly towns.[9]

The resumption of trade from the twelfth century increased commercial activity, feeding this capital accumulation in the cities. Trade over long distances cannot conveniently be carried out on a sustained and significant basis by barter or direct exchange, including exchanges with commodity money. Rather than direct exchanges, contracts were necessary to complete exchanges at future dates in distant locations. Beginning with the great medieval fairs at Champagne and elsewhere, a new kind of money came into being: money which was no longer a commodity of intrinsic value, but a contract, a promise, an instrument of debt. Security was transferred from certain physical objects to promises made by certain individuals. Instead of accepting only precious metals, people began to accept other people's IOUs in exchange for goods and services, on the assumption that they would be made good (cashed-in for commodity money) in the expected course of events. As IOUs were used more and more, they were increasingly taken for the money they represented. As a result, money slowly but steadily changed its meaning: it was gradually transformed from hard currency into a commitment to pay in the future, a personal contract, what we now call credit.[10] The two long coexisted—and still do—but credit has steadily replaced coinage. Merchants travelling to the great medieval fairs developed a system of promissory notes to facilitate their trades, and these evolved into bills of exchange—contracts by which merchants in different locations extended credit to one another, which in turn were paid off in local currencies, usually precious metals. As these claims for future payment—IOUs—began to circulate as a medium of exchange, what were personal notes (which might still bear personal seals or signatures) were gradually turned into impersonal ones, and ultimately into bank notes.

Since off-setting bills mostly cancelled out one another given the overall reciprocal flow of business between two centers, such as London and Amsterdam, only relatively small amounts of cash (coins) were required to settled final differences at each end. As bills were often passed to third parties and came to circulate more or less widely, they came to act as a kind of supplementary currency (much as checks do in a modern economy). Here we see the key shift in the meaning of money. As the volume of commerce increased, demand for credit increased. As the credit economy steadily expanded, the erosion and evasion of usury laws allowed for interest to be attached to more and more of this credit, promoting a new motive for further economic growth. Credit itself need not drive economic growth, though it is essential to any complex economy. Without it, for instance, capital projects could not be undertaken. What drives economic growth—and here we see the beginnings of the growth dynamic—is the crucial combination of credit *plus* interest for profit.

Other factors feeding this commercial revolution were at work as well. The Knights Templar, who started out as protectors of pilgrims going to the Holy Land, developed a shipping and trading network in the Mediterranean world during the Crusades. The Templers, still working within the context of usury laws, got most of their income from fees, but their far-flung network involving the Church, European princes and monarchs, and merchants and suppliers, created an early and far-flung demand for credit. At the same time the prohibition against usury slowly began to erode. Jews in the Middle Ages, exempt from usury laws, were able to charge interest on loans, setting an example envied by other would-be lenders. But it was only with the rise of Italian bankers—especially Lombards—beginning in the thirteenth century that interest was charged openly on loans by Christians. Sometimes offending bankers were excommunicated, but material profits began to outweigh such spiritual risks. The sea-change in this attitude only came, as we saw in the last chapter, with the triumph of the Reformation. It should be kept in mind, however, that these early credit precedents were developed in the context of what remained an overall subsistence economy, with most production still localized. Available credit remained limited, given the relatively small-scale (even if sometimes geographically widely dispersed) nature of most of the commercial activities of the period.

Before the implications of lending at interest could be developed on any significant scale, a sizable commercial economy was necessary. For that to happen, the subsistence economy, or significant parts of it, had to be monetized, that is, given a price and cleared through a market. Today this is something we take for granted; nearly everything we consume is purchased through commercial exchanges—we are mostly shoppers in acquiring goods and services—but in early modern Europe, as elsewhere in the pre-modern world, most people were peasants and artisans, that is, producers for whom the challenges of food, clothing, and shelter were solved mostly locally by local labor, and largely outside any cash economy as we know it. Cash that did exist was subordinate to, not dominant over, such exchanges. The late medieval village did not have a convenience store. Peasants and artisans were not shoppers, or rather so only at the margin, perhaps at the weekly marketplace or at the seasonal regional fair. They lived in small, close-knit communities bound more by the moral rather than the legal reciprocities of kinship and neighborhood. In a localized world with a long history of personal favors and courtesies (and animosities), the balance of give and take was not standardized, not reduced to a cash exchange, but was constantly shifting and endlessly nuanced.

This localized, sustainable world persisted far longer than we usually imagine. Traces of it can still be seen in Thomas Hardy's mostly rural novels of the late nineteenth century in England. A telling example can be found in this author's own region: rural upstate New York. The initial stages of settlement in the region, following the opening of the frontier, were indeed dependent on outside support to varying degrees, and the earliest settler communities were far from self-sufficient. But once established at a time when industrialization had not yet taken hold—the early to mid-nineteenth century—they naturally evolved into almost entirely self-sufficient communities. Historian Dominick J. Reisen makes this rather surprising point in discussing the small hamlet of Clarksville, NY, which might be taken as typical of many such rural communities across the United States:

> By the middle of the nineteenth century the people of Clarksville could be very proud of the state of their community and the level of self-sufficiency it had gained. Outward displays of prosperity were not only evident in the adornments both personal and architectural, that people used, but also in the ability to meet all of a person's basic needs. Indeed, by this time, the people in and around Clarksville could purchase anything they needed in the hamlet. The necessity to travel to neighboring communities for finished goods had nearly completely disappeared. Further, the rising level of wealth being created in Clarksville by these businessmen and their families was leading to a desire for ever more luxurious products. This need too was being served by the local businesses. By the mid-nineteenth century, for the first time, Clarksville represented a self-sufficient central New York community. [11]

What we see here, it seems, is an advanced form of self-sufficiency, rising even to the level of luxurious prosperity, not yet subsumed by commercial networks of communication, production, and distribution. Only with the railroad and the telegraph was this kind of localism finally breached, bringing to rural areas the broader trading networks developed earlier among larger urban centers.

The commercial revolution, the expansion of trade stimulated first by the Crusades, took off dramatically with the discovery of America, the opening of sea routes around Africa to south and east Asia, and the slave trade. Europe in 1500 was a relatively backward part of the world, as historians often remind us, with limited production compared to Asia, especially China and India. But what Europe did manage to achieve was control of the seas based on new shipping, navigation and gunnery technology. The Chinese, under the Ming dynasty in the fifteenth century, mounted extensive maritime expeditions to India and Africa, but abruptly discontinued them, leaving the field to the Europeans. This fateful withdrawal meant that the benefits of global trade—including the resources of the Americas—went to European, not Asian, merchants. Over time this new wealth was concentrated in the great trading cities of Italy and northwest Europe (especially the Low Countries), in places like Venice and Genoa, and later Bruges, Antwerp and Amsterdam. Similarly the cities of the Hanseatic League controlled the trade for natural resources in the Baltic and Eastern Europe. In spite of an overall negative balance in the principal trade with Asia, European merchants made money—lots of it. The commercial economy, established for the first time in northern Italy and Holland, and then in Britain, provided a context favorable to the use of money and credit. The medieval world of lords and peasants living on largely self-sustaining isolated manors or estates disappeared first in the Protestant countries of northwestern Europe, though it long lingered on in southern and eastern Europe.

By the seventeenth century the concentration of capital in Holland had reached a critical threshold. One noted historian of this golden age of Holland, Simon Schama, aptly titled his work *An Embarrassment of Riches*, capturing the astonishing novelty and success of the commercial revolution. The Dutch, it seems, more than anyone in the West since the palmy days of ancient Rome, had more money than they knew what to do with. They discovered, unlike the Romans, that the best use of money was to make more money. They invested it, mostly in overseas ventures, utilizing the innovation of the joint-stock company in which private investors could purchase shares, the most famous being the Dutch East India Company. These shares were traded through another Dutch innovation, the stock market. A further innovation was central banking. The first central bank is often said to have been the Wisselbank, the Exchange Bank of Amsterdam, a public bank founded in 1609. There were earlier banks, especially in Italy, but the Wisselbank, with its public backing, provided for a scale of operations and stability hitherto unmatched. Along with a number of subsidiary local banks, it performed central banking functions, though a formal central bank was not established in the Netherlands until 1814.[12] The Exchange Bank was soon followed (1614) by a lending bank. The Dutch, in short, had excess money to invest in speculative ventures, and the institutions to facilitate such investment. Perhaps the most notable manifestation of this new speculative state of mind was the famous tulip bubble of the 1630s.

Another important breakthrough toward a mature credit economy came with the foundation of the Dutch East India Company—the first great modern corporation—early in the seventeenth century. Prior to this time, most overseas commerce was funded on a voyage-by-voyage basis, with investors organized into ad hoc groups which dissolved after each project. The genius of the Dutch East India Company was to offer to investors perpetual shares in an ongoing company, the first significant joint-stock company in Europe. Shares could not be redeemed, but, like medieval annuities, they could be bought from and sold to third parties. In addition shareholders were paid regular dividends (at a high rate). Control of the company, moreover, was confined to the management, with the shareholders in effect silent partners.[13] The result was a well-run enterprise whose shares were in constant demand;

this dovetailed nicely with the Amsterdam stock market (the *Beurs*), the first real stock market in Europe. Similar stock markets soon appeared in London and elsewhere (Frankfort, Paris). In the seventeenth century hundreds of joint-stock companies, for domestic as well as foreign commerce, were created and traded on these exchanges, though only a few persisted for long. The Wisselbank of Amsterdam—"wissel" meaning bill of exchange—was founded to meet the demand for deposits and transfer payments arising not only from the use of bills of exchange, but also to facilitate transactions in the new stock markets. This combination of institutions made Holland the financial capital of Europe. The concentration of wealth was phenomenal. In the years between its founding in 1602 and its close in 1796, the Dutch East India Company, the largest corporation for most of this era, "averaged an annual payout of 18 percent on its original capital,"[14] an astronomical return by any standard anywhere.

The Netherlands was a small country; more a series of confederated city states than a nation-state. As historian Richard Ehrenberg notes,

> The Republic of the United Netherlands was pre-eminently an association of towns. Its credit in the first place rested on that of the individual provinces, and this again on that of the towns. Every town and every province formed a corporation whose members the burghers were associated together for their benefit, even if they were no longer (like the burghers of earlier times) liable both in their persons and their goods as sureties for the debts of the community.

He continues:

> in the province of Holland alone there were 65,000 who had or were able to invest money in annuities. It is just this large number of world-be investors that is the most powerful force with which we have to do here. For once this had made it possible for the Netherlands, not only to borrow in their own country, but also to purchase foreign assistance. This made it possible to treat the State debt from the beginning as a funded one, to employ the old plan of the sale of annuities, and in this way to ensure that the creditors had no right of calling in as well as the low rate of interest.[15]

The Dutch, in short, invented the first system of national public credit. For the first time in European and, it appears, world history, we find a credit system not dependent solely on the vicissitudes of private bankers like the Medici or the Fuggers and their unreliable private debtors, like the monarchs of Europe. Credit was now backed by publically guaranteed, more or less perpetual national institutions. The bourse and the bank of Amsterdam had behind them the imprimatur of the collective corporate backing of the provinces and towns.

Although this financial power enabled the Dutch to win their independence from Spain through a long war of independence, by the later seventeenth century they suffered a series of naval defeats at British hands, ending their freedom of action. Yet Holland remained in many respects the financial center of Europe throughout the eighteenth century, and for the most part entered into a kind of economic symbiosis with the British. The Glorious Revolution of 1688 put a Dutchman, William of Orange, on the British throne, and London financial markets thereafter became a favorite of Dutch investors. The defeat of the Catholic Stuarts was in part the work of the Dutch, allied with important Protestant factions in Britain, who aimed to stave off an alliance between a Catholic Britain and a Catholic France which would have been a direct threat to Holland and its commercial interests. Politically and economically, though not at first financially, the Dutch became junior partners to the British. As late at the 1760s, Dutch shipping carried three times the tonnage of British shipping.[16] The persistence of Dutch power even in the late eighteenth century was demonstrated by their support of the American revolutionaries in their struggle with Britain. As one financial historian puts it:

> The jig was up when Dutch investors, long a great prop to the British capital markets, slowed their purchases of British bonds, making 'a pretty general refusal . . . to subscribe' to British loans, and began to buy American ones. Dutch complicity in the American victory was no coincidence. The Dutch saw in America themselves, republicans struggling mightily against a massive, distant, imperial overlord.[17]

The survival of the Dutch lay in the successful export to Britain made friendly to them of the essentials of their financialized economic system, in access to British capital markets, and in the protection thereby of their own assets. In the words of historian John Brewer,

> eighteenth century English finance worked on a seventeenth century Dutch model: it used a public bank to handle the loans, based the debt on long-term redeemable annuities, and spread the debt among a substantial number of borrowers. The precise links between the English eighteenth-century financial revolution and the Dutch system of public funding which originated in the Hapsburg Netherlands in the mid-sixteenth century have never been established. But the similarities are so great, the obsession of English ministers with Dutch methods so well known, and the arrival of William III and his Dutch advisors so timely, that it is hard to believe that contemporaries were wrong when they described the new financial arrangements as 'Dutch finance.'[18]

But this transposition was not a cut and dried affair. A good case could be made that the commercial revolution, which was brought to a climax by the Dutch, provided an alternative road in important respects *not* taken by subsequent British, Western, and world financial history. The Dutch were unique in having a powerful system of public finance in which a largely democratic government bypassed private banks and dealt directly with ordinary citizens, issuing both short-term and long-term debt, as well as annuities denominated in small amounts to attract small investors. The principal historians of Dutch finance and capitalism of this era, J. de Vries and S. van der Woude, call this a form of "popular capitalism."[19] Gradually, it is true, bondholding became concentrated in fewer and fewer hands,[20] leading to the creation of a small and increasingly parasitical rentier class. As so often is the case, technical decisions about the arcana of finance, in this case, how to market debt, gave the advantage to larger debt-holders. If there is to be a viable form of public credit, it will require a greater degree of transparency and simplicity than has been common in financial history, even in Holland. We will entertain a system which purports to meet those criteria in chapter seven. Nonetheless, the Dutch achievement was remarkable.

The Dutch developed sophisticated financial institutions in the context not only of representative government, but of decentralized local autonomy, which is the essence of the real political democracy that is the necessary complement to economic democracy. The various Dutch states, even before they gained their independence from the Hapsburgs, gained the power to collect and control taxation, resisting attempts to centralize fiscal authority. This decentralized structure persisted throughout the history of the Republic of the United Netherlands, as the Dutch state was officially called. The Republic was a loose association of seven states, minimally formalized by the Union of Utrecht in 1579. All seven states had to agree to common financial matters. The success of trade and commerce gave the Dutch the largest money supply of any European country. This pool of capital ensured relatively low interest rates. Given the widespread distribution of public debt, what de Vries and van der Woude call "the first modern economy" managed to achieve, if not quite an egalitarian society, was at least one in which wealth was widely held and prosperity enjoyed by the bulk of society. Visitors during the Dutch golden age were astonished to find oil paintings in peasant houses in the countryside; and analyses of probate records reveal large amounts of cash commonly left at death, even by members of the lower classes.[21]

Because the Republic avoided both the centralization and the privatization of national finance, as occurred later in Britain, and because interest rates remained relatively low, it was able to tolerate a mildly usurious financial system. In the Dutch system the imperatives of usurious finance were never wholly institutionalized, hence the compulsion to economic "growth" was—in spite of the great wealth of the Dutch states—never built into the financial and economic system. Interestingly, no mechanism for issuing currency was ever established either, leaving the Dutch economy rooted not in the elastic debt-currencies of the future, but in the commodity monies of the past. In the words of de Vries and van der Woude, "The absence of institutional modifications to accommodate the growth of credit, the absence of a bank of issue, and the systematic bias of banking houses against the interests of investors, all contributed to the ultimate failure of Amsterdam as a major financial center."[22]

One might comment that this was a failure which took two centuries to become manifest, and then only by outside force. The Dutch Republic, after all, fell in the end only due to the overwhelming power of an energized revolutionary and Napoleonic France, not because of its internal weaknesses. Further, de Vries and van der Woude are measuring the "failure" of the Republic against the dominant usurious financial system which replaced it. We might instead consider that the Dutch brought the commercial revolution as close to perfection as anyone, and that the system which succeeded it was a tragic step backward. De Vries and van der Woude themselves seem to recognize, in the very last words of their book, that the Dutch Republic did not lead to perpetual "growth" and that "the first modern economy" it created can be read as a model for a steady-state economy: ". . . modern economic growth is no process of growth without end but rather tends at some point towards deceleration and stagnation. A first cycle of such growth, crisis, and stagnation was pioneered by the Netherlands between the sixteenth century and 1850; a second cycle, affecting the whole western world, began between 1780 and 1850. When will it end? This we cannot answer, but the situation in which the old Republic found itself in the early eighteenth century seems in many ways illustrative of the problems of today."[23]

NOTES

1. Henri Pirenne, *Economic and Social History of Medieval Europe* (London: Routledge & Kegan Paul, 1953), p. 113

2. Ibid., pp. 7–8.

3. E. Lipson, *The Economic History of England* (London: Adam and Charles Black, 1959), pp. 88ff.

4. For a detailed account of the financial collapse of European monarchs see Richard Ehrenberg, *Capital and Finance in the Age of the Renaissance* [1928] (reprint, Fairfield, NJ: Augustus Kelley, 1985), *et. passim*.

5. Niall Ferguson, *The Ascent of Money* (New York: Penguin, 2008), p. 74.

6. Christopher Hollis, *The Two Nations* (New York: Gordon Press, 1975), p, 10.

7. Robert E. Wright, *One Nation Under Debt* (New York: McGraw Hill, 2008), p. 19.

8. Niall Ferguson, *The Ascent of Money* (New York: Penguin, 2008), pp. 71–2.

9. Ehrenberg, *Capital and Finance in the Age of the Renaissance* [1928] (reprint, Fairfield, NJ: Augustus Kelley, 1985) pp. 53–4.

10. For a general account of the history of credit, see Scott B. MacDonald and Albert L. Gastmann, *A History of Credit and Power in the Western World* (New Brunswick, Transaction Publishers, 2001); I largely follow their narrative here.

11. Dominick J. Reisen, *Middlefield and the Settling of the New York Frontier* (Voorheesville: Square Circle Press, 2009), p. 162.

12. See *Wikipedia*, "Financial History of the Dutch Republic," http://en.wikipedia.org/wiki/Financial_history_of_the_Dutch_Republic.

13. See Larry Neal, *The Rise of Financial Capitalism: International Capital Markets in the Age of Reason* (Cambridge: Cambridge University Press, 1990), p. 8–9 et *passim*.

14. Ibid., p. 17.

15. Ehrenberg, op. cit., pp. 349–50.

16. Niall Ferguson, *The Ascent of Money* (New York: Penguin, 2008), p. 136.

17. Robert E. Wright, *One Nation Under Debt* (New York: McGraw Hill, 2008), pp. 64–5.

18. John Brewer, *The Sinews of Power* (Cambridge: Harvard University Press, 1990), p. 133.

19. J. de Vries and A. van der Woude, *The First Modern Economy* (Cambridge: Cambridge University Press, 1997), p. 116.

20. Ibid., p. 115.

21. Ibid., p. 88.

22. Ibid., p. 158.

23. Ibid., pp. 721–2.

Chapter Four

The Financial Revolution

It was in Britain that "Dutch finance" took a new and fateful twist, one with enormous consequences. There financial institutions had been less developed. The distractions of the English Civil War, Cromwell's rule, and the Restoration prevented the degree of financial development achieved earlier in Holland. Charles II had defaulted on the royal debt in the 1672, and naval conflicts with the Dutch and French further strained English finances. Furthermore, Britain, a much larger and more integrated country with a more consistent history of independence than Holland, faced the crucial challenge of incorporating a large-scale agricultural hinterland with the commercial activities of the City of London. Nonetheless, beginning with a 1665 Act of Parliament conceived by the ingenious George Downing, an Exchequer official under Charles II, the precedent was established which required "Parliament to guarantee that loans made to the King . . . should be repaid with interest, in strict rotation, out of specially earmarked funds."[1] Later, with the influx of commercially-minded Huguenots into Britain following Louis XIV's revocation of the Edict of Nantes in 1685, followed by the Glorious Revolution and the entry of Dutch financial interests into British affairs after 1689, the stage was set for institutionalizing the public debt. This was no less than a transformation of British finance, symbolized by the founding of the Bank of England in 1694. It was left to Britain, not Holland, to achieve the final and fateful breakthrough of the financial revolution: the establishment of credit-creating, interest-charging institutions run for private profit with taxpayer backing. The Bank of Amsterdam, historian Pierre Vilar reminds us, ". . . was not . . . a credit institution: it did not give advances, or discount bills or notes; in principle, deposits had to cover any transactions in which the party was concerned, and therefore no credit was given."[2] Although it did begin to create some limited credit after 1683,[3] it was only with the establishment of the Bank of England that a genuine and significant for-profit (that is, usurious) credit-creating banking institution was established.

It was the London goldsmiths in the mid-seventeenth century who exploited the idea that money could be created literally out of nothing when they realized that only a small percentage of depositors at any point were likely to actually demand their money back. The Swedish Riksbank apparently made the same discovery about the same time,[4] and some fractional reserve operations were known in Holland, but it was the goldsmiths of London, not the Swedes or the Dutch, who influenced subsequent financial history by their use of fractional reserve banking. They realized that new money (a lot of it) could be created by making loans at full value on a mere fractional basis–a principal incorporated into the Bank of England and subsequent modern banking. Charles II, desperate to raise funds to fight wars against the Dutch and the French, and eager to avoid further indebtedness to the goldsmiths, hit upon another novel expedient: issuing his own paper currency. A struggle ensued with the goldsmiths, whose monetary monopoly was now threatened by the King. Since Charles issued only notes of large denominations people took them to the goldsmiths to exchange for more convenient, smaller denominated notes, which they supplied but only on condition of discounting Charles' notes, which fell in price significantly, thereby calling their value into question. Charles as a result was unable to redeem his notes, and stopped payment in 1672. Many goldsmiths, because they held so many of Charles' notes, were thereby dragged into bankruptcy. Each side blamed the other, and a war of words developed in pamphlets and broadsides. The private interests regrouped and, with continued Dutch support, were able to blame the monarchy for the financial meltdown, setting the stage for the struggle with James II which led to the Glorious Revolution. Any chance for establishing public finance in Britain was killed. In the end the Stuarts–Charles and his brother James, who succeeded him–lost the game when the Dutch backed the opposition of the London money markets to James, whose unpopular Catholic faith undercut his support in the land.

In the so-called Glorious Revolution of 1688 James was forced into exile and his protestant nephew, William of Orange, became King of England with the backing of the opposition to James. There would be no question now of a public credit system to the advantage of the king and the public. What evolved instead, after some debate and experimentation, was a peculiar hybrid, pregnant with historical significance: a privatized credit system backed by public tax revenues. The essence of the new system was the creation of money through usurious lending to the public and to the government by a privatized central bank, which was given a monopoly on issuing government debt or notes as legal tender in return for providing the government with much needed funding. In the words of one financial historian, "what had been created by the incorporation [of the Bank of England] was something more precious than cash, and that was credit."[5] Usurious credit, that is. The Bank of England, established by an act of Parliament in 1694, assumed the personal debt of the monarch, turning it into a national debt. But though the debt was national–subject to repayment by the government through funds collected through taxation—the bank, in spite of its name, was privately owned by its 1500 or so investors, a sizable number of them Dutch. Instead of depending on the whims of its depositors, like earlier banks (other than the Wisselbank), the Bank of England was backed by the taxing power of the state, which stood ready to guarantee payments of government bonds; this made it far more secure, and, as we might say, "too big to fail." But it was the bank and its investors who pocketed the interest on those bonds and other loans while evading any significant public accountability for their policies. Its notes, payments to borrowers, circulated as legal tender–British pounds— and gradually became the dominant currency of the land.

Here's how one historian sums up the deal that put the new system into practice:

> The plan was that, instead of borrowing from the goldsmiths, the Government should instead borrow £1,200,000, of which it was in need, from a newly formed Corporation called the Bank of England. This corporation promised to collect the required money from the public and to lend it on to the King at 8 percent plus £4000 per annum for expenses—a rate considerably lower than that which he would have had to pay to the goldsmiths. In return for lending at this low rate the Bank received a number of privileges of which the most important was that it had the right to issue notes up to the extent of its loan to the Government 'under their common seal' on the security of the Government. This it to say, it had the right to issue a £1 note; the holder of that £1 note had the right to demand that the Bank give him cash for his note, but, if he made that demand, the Bank had the right to demand that the Government raise that £1 by taxation and repay £1 worth of debt to the Bank so that the Bank might repay its £1 to the note-holder. As Disraeli put it, 'the principle of that system was to mortgage industry in order to protect property' or, as Paterson, the originator of the Bank, himself explained with charming simplicity, 'The bank hath benefit of the interest on all moneys which it creates out of nothing.'[6]

The notes put into circulation by the bank were literally created out of nothing since the money they represented had already been loaned to the government and spent on military and other expenses. But since it was owed back to the bank by the government, it could stand as collateral for further notes issued by the bank, that is, a further round of lending, this time to the public. The key idea—a most ingenious invention—was to use old debts as collateral for new ones, and to put these new notes, or debt-money, into circulation as the currency of the nation. The original money put up by the bank's investors—the £1,200,000 which first funded the bank—may have been directly or indirectly commodity money, but the notes issued on the collateral of the debt held by the bank after lending to the government were simply promissory notes lent out at interest. These notes could be converted into cash upon demand, but since they functioned as money in every other way, and had the imprimatur of the state behind them, the incentive for demanding cash—that is, some form of commodity money—faded away. Credit money replaced commodity money for all practical purposes. The tether to commodity money to be sure was maintained for centuries afterwards by the gold standard, until it was abandoned in the twentieth century, but the fundamental shift to credit (at usurious rates) had nonetheless been accomplished.

The financial revolution in England, first put on the historical map by P. G. M. Dickson in his pioneering classic work of the same name published in 1967, was not confined to the invention of usurious debt money by the Bank of England. An additional ingredient was the development of the first real securities market in the world, within which the bank played a central role. (A few other financial institutions, including the South Seas Company, the East India Company, and the Million Bank, played similar roles in facilitating the circulation of credit, though the Bank of England came to dominate the field.) Dickson puts the importance of securities markets this way:

> For unless facilities had existed to enable lenders to sell to a third party their claim on the state to annual interest, the government's system of long-term borrowing would never have got off the ground. The state would have been obliged to promise repayment in a limited number of years—and to keep their promise. This would have effectually stopped it from borrowing on the scale it needed. The rise of the market solved the dilemma by—to adapt a Keynesian phrase—making debts that were permanent for the state liquid for the individual; subject only to the risk of capital loss if market prices fell.[7]

This system was made permanent by the recognition that the national debt never had to be repaid, but could be continually turned over by selling new securities to replace those coming due.

A small group of historians, including John Brewer and Richard Bonney, have followed in Dickson's footsteps emphasizing the importance of the financial revolution, but the work of this group has had little impact beyond a relatively narrow scholarly circle. As a result, the profound importance of the financial revolution for our own time has been missed by historians, commentators, public policy analysts, and the general public. Brewer has argued that the financial revolution in England was closely related to the massive demands made by seventeenth century European warfare, resulting in what he calls the "fiscal-military state." Typical European armies in the seventeenth century, he points out, exploded in size by a factor of ten.[8] The major powers could not afford to ignore this escalation and those that did, such as the Polish-Lithuanian Commonwealth, suffered decline and ultimate extinction. "The state's military role," Brewer writes of Britain, as well as its competitors, "made it the most important single factor in the domestic econo-my."[9] We tend to think of early modern European states, including Britain, as having predominately civilian commercial and agricultural economies, but Brewer's sharp correction reminds us that warfare (actual or potential) was a key economic factor then, as now.

This world of relentless warfare, escalated by new military methods and technologies, put an unprecedented strain on state finances. Apart from the new financial techniques pioneered in Holland, most early modern European states were mired in a patchwork of feudal arrangements which made direct taxation difficult, and restricted state (that is, royal) revenues to what could be negotiated from powerful aristocrats, independent cities and towns, and other insulated groups, as well as what could be extracted directly from royal estates. These feudal arrangement turned out not to be enough to meet the new financial demands. Monarchs were often reduced to expedients, such as the sale of offices and tax farming, to raise desperately needed cash to support armies and navies, falling further and further into unsustainable debt. Of the more important powers, England had perhaps the most centralized government, was least feudal in its social structure, and, next to Holland, had the most advanced commercial economy. The significance of the financial revolution which was brought to maturity in England was that she was the first and for a long time the only large European state to solve this problem. She alone in the eighteenth century through the financial revolution was able to mobilize her wealth to support her military, above all her navy, without bankrupting herself, and the solution she pioneered has become a mainstay of modern governments ever since. As Brewer puts it: " . . . the ease with which substantial sums were raised is attributable to three circumstances: the existence of a powerful representative with undisputed powers of national taxation; the presence of a commercialized economy whose structure made it comparatively simple to tax; and the deployment of fiscal expertise that made borrowing against tax income an easy tax."[10]

The financial revolution not only allowed Britain to fund its military forces, it allowed it also to fund its commercial economy on a level and scale hitherto unimaginable. One last quote from Brewer, on the eighteenth century English economy gives the measure of the financial revolution:

> Credit was everywhere. Contemporaries estimated that two-thirds of all trans-actions involved credit rather than cash. Surviving inventories indicate the importance of borrowing and lending. In a recent study of wealth in pre-industrial Cumbria, 30 percent of a sample of local yeoman had 50 percent or more of their assets out in credit. At the other end of the country, in Petworth in Sussex, between a third and a half of local tradesmen 'were filling the useful function of bankers, tiding neighbors over bad crops and fires, enabling them to acquire their own houses or restock a farm.' Such medium and long-term loans were paralleled by short-term credit which was the lubricant that

> smoothed most commercial transactions. . . . the circulating capital of most
> eighteenth-century businesses, which took the form of stock and trade debts,
> was usually four or five times greater than fixed assets. Trade without credit
> was an impossibility.[11]

By the early eighteenth century in Britain, then, we see the results of the novel Dutch-British financial symbiosis, with Dutch capital and techniques taken up and combined with British innovations such as privatized fractional reserve banking and effective securities markets. This new credit economy, once injected into Britain, slowly but steadily transformed a series of local economies based on land and traditional methods of production into a national economy based on credit and untraditional methods of production. Once this new credit economy was established, it took but a few decades to fully absorb and transform the old traditional economy, and to subject it to a steady pressure to grow, a pressure which first affected agriculture, and then manufacturing, as these sectors increasingly came to depend on credit. Under this pressure manufacturers were forced to innovate, and the factory and the industrial system was the result. Of course this new economy was a *usurious* credit economy. The great modern invention of credit was from the start subjected to what the church had called the "sin" of usury.

The credit economy was given a new and fateful twist in Britain. Instead of a system of public credit avoiding usury, which the Dutch pioneered, British financial interests opted for a privatized for-profit usurious credit system backed by the state. A new investor class arose, combining the old landed wealth of the aristocracy with the new financial opportunities pioneered by bankers and merchants in commercial centers like Amsterdam and London. Since it invented the credit system, and few others understood it (then as now), this new investor class was able to privatize and perpetuate it in its own and not the public's interest. Dickson had no hesitation is calling this class from the beginning a "plutocracy."[12] There were some important exceptions during this period to this privatization and exploitation of finance—the public status of the Bank of Amsterdam, as we have seen, as well as the paper currencies of the contemporary British American colonies—but such experiments in public finance for the public good were soon marginalized as usurious private banking became dominant in Britain, and eventually in America, and subsequently over much of the world.

The financial revolution was not only the bridge between the new commercial economy and the industrial revolution; it was also the key to modernity. Once the financial revolution took place, wealth was redefined in terms of money, that is, the credit system, with land no longer its primary measure. Land, because of the crops and livestock it can support through renewable solar energy, is inherently productive, but only on a more or less steady basis within fixed limits. If it is decent land it will have some natural rate of surplus, given some application of labor and technology. And that rate will be more or less constant over time, depending as it does on renewable resources. Money by contrast has no natural rate of surplus; it can be invested wisely, put in a mattress, or squandered. To be productive it must be translated into something material which does have a natural rate of production. If no interest is charged, as we shall see later, then the rate of return will actually be negative; it will be less than the replacement rate needed just to keep things going at a steady state, not to mention a growth rate. But if lenders insist on a usurious rate of interest, that is, on *an extra return above and beyond current rates of production*, as they were in a position to do after the English financial revolution built in usurious expectations of return on investment, they in effect impose upon the economy the burden of expanding production beyond what is constant and replenishable. Instead of investment being dictated by reality, reality now became subject to the command of investment. There is no other way to repay a loan with interest, after all, than to use that loan somehow to stimulate not only the same rate of production, *but an additional rate of production*, or to get someone else to do it. Only in this way could the surplus required for repayment of both principal and interest be secured.

This new system of finance established first in Britain in the early eighteenth century is well summed up by one monetary historian, Glyn Davies, in a passage worth contemplating:

> The fact that more than half of the total money supply was now being created, not by the mint under the dictate of the monarch, but rather by the London money market and the provincial bankers gave rise to the most profound constitutional consequences. First, in order to carry out his much more burdensome civil and military duties, the monarch, after a painful but vain struggle, had been forced to call parliaments regularly. Secondly, because of the state's need to supplement taxes . . . the state had been forced to take into account the views and interests of the moneyed classes and the nature of the institutions which its borrowing had very largely brought into being. The national debt not only created the Bank of England but also virtually created the London money and capital markets in recognizable modern form long before an equity market in industrial shares became of importance. Provided that the government's general policy was acceptable in the City, the government's sources of finance, though no longer directly under its control, had been enormously increased. Trevelyan's traditional view that 'the financial system that arose after the Revolution [of 1688] was key to the power of England in the eighteenth and nineteenth centuries' . . . is strongly supported by modern research. Thus P. G. M. Dickson in his detailed study of the development of public credit from 1688 to 1756 shows how these fiscal changes in stimulating the growth of the London money and capital markets financed external imperialism as well as internal economic growth. [13]

This from a thorough historian, albeit one not only largely uncritical of, but even enthusiastic about, this financial revolution. Like many other scholars, Davies takes these portentous financial developments for granted as a step in human progress. In his mainstream narrative, the control of money is pried loose from "the sovereign power" who exercised it "ostentatiously and visibly," and is replaced by "market forces," characterized by Adam Smith's "invisible hand." Davies goes on, waxing eloquent:

> Ordinary people, 'peddlers turned merchants', drovers of cattle, innkeepers, iron masters, linen makers, shopkeepers, indeed almost any Tom, Dick or Harry could now share the royal prerogative. This was an unconscious, unplanned and still underestimated transfer of constitutional sovereignty; a partial financial democratization that preceded and facilitated the advent of democracy.[14]

Davies is surely right that that this remains an underestimated transfer of sovereignty over the money supply. But he is far from the mark in claiming that "almost any Tom, Dick or Harry" could now share the royal prerogative in creating money. This power went rather to a very small number of people, a plutocratic oligarchy based in the City of London, perhaps best defined by the 1500 or so initial individual shareholders in the Bank of England, including members of the royal family. Though some 60,000 individuals eventually held public funds in Britain by the 1760s,[15] this remained a very small percentage of the population, and even among this group a relatively small number held a disproportionate share of the funds. Wresting monetary power from the sovereign meant wresting it from the public realm; it meant privatizing in a few hands what used to be a public function. Royal sovereignty wasn't democratic, to be sure, but at least it was coextensive with the public sphere and recognizably accountable to it, particularly in terms of feudal traditions and obligations.

The new financial plutocracy was bound by no such traditions and responsibilities, and was noticeably less accountable to the public than old royal regimes. The metaphor of Smith's 'invisible hand' suggests, after all, a lack of transparency and accountability. Nor is there anything democratic about it. Democracy is surely about accountability to the public, which is precisely what the financial revolution obscured with regard to money and credit. Monetary policy in "the English system," subsequently adopted in America (by the followers of Alexander Hamilton) and lately in many parts of the world, is set not by any accountable public assembly, but by private interests. And finally, Tom, Dick, and Harry, far from being liberated by the privatization of national finance, found themselves subject to the risks of debt servitude to private interests. The coinage of the monarch was limited by supplies of precious metals expected in most final payments of obligations, but at least it was interest-free. Now all that changed. After the financial revolution and in most places where its commercial writ ran, credit (that is, borrowed money) could be had by many (because it now freely and legally could be created), but only at interest. The age of usury had begun.

This financial revolution has not gone entirely unnoticed by historians, though they have mostly missed its full depth and fateful significance. It is perhaps noteworthy that the pioneering work on the financial revolution, P. G. M. Dickson's *Financial Revolution in England*, is out of print today. David Armitage writes:

> The Financial Revolution in England—first so called by P. G. M. Dickson in 1967—was a late-comer onto the historiographical stage. . . . The undeniable fact that by the mid-eighteenth century England had grown from a bystander in European power-politics to the major player demands explanation: the strength of Britain's institutions of public finance and revenue-collection provides a large part of the answer.

Armitage goes on to tell us that the struggle between England and France "demanded the commitment of huge resources of blood and, especially, treasure. Taken together, the institutional innovations compelled by those wars amounted to a revolution in public finance which took off in the 1690s."[16] Armitage makes the point that these new wars were not over territory and dynastic and religious considerations, as in the past, but over control of trade. They were among the first wars spawned by the new commercial economy. "To finance such conflicts," Armitage notes, "took both excise revenue and, pre-eminently, an unparalleled system of public credit. The expansion of trade, which would increase the excise, and the creation of the Bank of England, which would underwrite the National Debt, were accordingly leading ideas . . ."[17] It was Britain which won this struggle, and it did so by consolidating and transforming the system of public finance pioneered in Holland. But this was more than the triumph of one great power over another; it was the birth of modernity itself, with its fateful Faustian bargain demanding economic growth at any price.

The implications of the new system were hardly evident at first. As the system of public credit became established, interest rates tended to drop; they dipped to 3 percent in Amsterdam by the late seventeenth century, and stayed at that level in Britain in the middle decades of the eighteenth century, once the crisis of the South Seas bubble was past.[18] Capital accumulation from trade combined with new credit markets meant an increase in liquidity; the more money available the less interest could be charged, but the difference was made up in volume. These initially lower rates (compared, say, to the double-digit rates of many Renaissance bankers) masked the implications of the suspension of usury laws in much of Europe. Once production is monetized in terms of a for-profit credit-based exchange economy, interest rates become vital. As long as interest rates are low, though still usurious, credit is relatively cheap and usually readily obtainable, widely distributed, and generally advantageous to the borrower, *especially given prospects for growth.* But once rates begin to climb, credit becomes harder to get, and wealth is concentrated in fewer hands—those of the creditors.

The high interest rates often charged in earlier eras were not of such great consequence because the lord in his manor, the peasants in their fields, and the artisans in their guilds and shops stood in important respects outside the credit economy, buffered as they were by feudal rights and duties, exchanges in kind, local production, fixed prices, guild regulations, access to the commons, and traditional customs and prerogatives. Princes often had trouble with creditors over money borrowed for war, as we have seen, but they could default without serious penalty, as Edward III of England and others did. Most people were not directly affected by these financial tumults. Edward III's bankruptcy in the fourteenth century was not England's bankruptcy. Many of the necessities of life in early modern Europe, it cannot be overemphasized, continued to be locally produced under local control. Markets were important, but largely supplemental. In the modern industrial economy, by contrast, markets and the credit to lubricate them are everything; they are inherently centralized and impersonal, and it is local, subsistence production which has been marginalized.

As long as money was a commodity with intrinsic value—preeminently gold or silver coins—the exchanges in which it was used were fully reciprocal and complete, even if deferred by credit; the coin received, immediately or later, was a value in hand equivalent to the goods or services rendered. The receipt of such money closed the transaction. But with the rise of token money—bills of exchange, certificates, and paper money generally—the money received was *not* of equivalent value in itself to goods and services rendered, but merely a token of such value, hopefully redeemable for actual value in the future. With token money exchanges are never really closed, but easily and thereby often endlessly deferred. The establishment in Britain of a perpetual national debt effectively institutionalized the endless deferral of debt. Commodity monies are media of exchange valuable in themselves, and represent no debt; their convenience allows them to universalize exchanges, and thereby, as we have seen, they perfect (but do not transcend) the barter system. Token monies, however, though also media of exchange, are also something very different. They are inherently promises of future redemption, and thereby they are credit/debt instruments.

Money as credit is full or mature money; we can call it "credit money" or "token money" (as opposed to commodity money). Credit money is a mere symbol, itself of little if any intrinsic value—a piece of paper, an electronic trace. It is a lawfully recognized token of a claim on existing resources, that is, legal tender. Money as credit, insofar as it transcends equivalent exchanges, allows us to claim resources *without* offering directly in return an equivalent value for them. This is as it should be, for only in this way do we gain access not otherwise possible to resources in anticipation of future needs, that is, for capital expenditures we can't make out of current cash flow. This is its great advantage over commodity money. Credit money does this while also functioning as a medium of exchange for current needs. But credit money, it cannot be overemphasized, does not have to be usurious. *What is needed, as we shall see, is a monetary system which provides much needed credit, that is, money, without the burden of unsustainable usury.* It is the tragedy and original sin, as it were, of the financial revolution that usury was attached to credit, and that subsequent economic development was not only skewed to the benefit of the few at the expense of the many, but that, because of its incessant demand for "growth," it proceeded without regard for replacing the resources it was depleting. The result is the combination of massive debt burdens and ecological overshoot we face today.

One of the most baleful effects of the financial revolution has been to destroy old commonly held forms of wealth without putting new ones in their place. Relentless and radical privatization, continuing to this day, decimated important communal structures. Before the financial revolution, at least in Western Europe, not only was land the major form of wealth, it was to a significant degree still held in common, side by side with various private holdings. The old commons in land was held by the community, generally the village, and used if not collectively, then at least according to collectively established rules. The traditional medieval commons was usually some mixture of pasture, field, and woodland, to which all members of the community had varying rights of access and usage, though we should bear in mind that such commons generally existed in the context of an overriding local authority, a lord or bishop, to whom village disputes were referred, and who enjoyed private possession of his own lands. Peasants or villeins were mostly under the authority of their lord, while freeholders, though technically under the lord's jurisdictions as well, had more options and sometimes had access to the King's courts. Peasants and freeholders utilized the commons collectively, but individually they farmed small private holdings of their own—all this in addition to the labor required of them on the lands of the lord or church. The medieval commons, respected by local authorities as necessary for the survival of the peasants, provided an important if less than complete buffer against exactions by princes and churchmen. But with the steady monetization of the economy in early modern Europe, the old commons was gradually marginalized and finally disappeared.

The old localized system of subsistence production supported by access to the commons was slowly but steadily eroded by the commercialization of agriculture, particularly by the raising of sheep for cash; it was not finally destroyed, however, until the new comprehensive system of national credit created and controlled by private, for-profit investors had triumphed. The privatization of land was most dramatically expressed in the enclosure movement in Britain. In two large waves, first in the fifteenth and sixteen centuries, and then more dramatically in the eighteenth and early nineteenth centuries, privatized commercial agriculture in Britain replaced much of the old open field system of the commons. By the end of the process, peasants and small freeholders had lost their old communal rights and culture, and became a new, fragmented underclass. They were driven into tenant farming, or wage-labor, whether on large estates in the country or in the new factories in the cities. Loss of the old commons, it was widely lamented, eliminated one of the last bulwarks against the impoverishment of the rural laboring classes.[19] The one-time peasant prosperity of the Middle Ages was lost forever. Once brought under private control, agricultural lands not only *could be* developed more efficiently, they, no less than manufactures, *had to be* so developed to the extent that money had to be borrowed to buy and clear land, to implement new techniques, etc. Land was incorporated into the new financial system through a variety of new instruments which facilitated investment: mortgages, liens, rents, fee simple ownership, etc. The result was the industrialization of agriculture, its transformation into an extractive enterprise culminating in the agri-business and mega-farms of today.

In Britain, in the eighteenth century, the new credit economy finally swallowed the traditional land economy and the last vestiges of the commons. It is important to recognize that it did not have to be that way. The potential for a new commons of non-profit credit, based on the public function of money and lending, was nipped in the bud by the privatization of the financial system. Credit could have replaced land as the new commons. That could have been the outcome of the financial revolution. But it didn't happen. Here is the key point: Those shut out from the land could have been compensated by gaining access to resources through some of the newly invented instruments of credit, and by debt-based money in particular, but the new credit was high-jacked almost from the start by shrewd interests who exploited it for private gain at the expense of public benefit. There is no reason why a financial system must be private not public. Even well-educated people to this day often believe that money is somehow issued by the state, though it is not. The coins of traditional monarchs, from Croesus to Louis XVI, were indeed state money, but that is now a quaint and distant memory. There is no reason in principle why governments should not issue the new form of modern money—credit—for the public good, provided we have democratic, accountable governments, which we do not today. This would be a way to restore a public commons—a truly people's money—a point we shall explore in detail in chapter seven.

Attempts to restore the commons in some form have characterized much of the resistance to "the English system" as it spread to other countries. These attempts, whether revolutionary or reformist, almost invariably invoked state power to appropriate and redistribute private wealth, whether in a limited fashion, as in the liberalism of the New Deal and the welfare state, or in wholesale fashion as in the communist states of the twentieth century. But state power in any form has not been able to restore the commons. The idea that resources can be recommunalized by government has turned out to be a dubious proposition at best. The aim of redistributive statists has been to take wealth from the rich, whether mildly through taxes or violently through revolution and confiscation of property, and distribute it to the poor. It hasn't worked. The state in these efforts reserved for itself the decision-making which in the commons had belonged to the people. Governments—even the representative governments of the so-called modern democracies—have become independent and largely unaccountable powers in themselves, either appropriating wealth for their own purposes (the military-industrial complex, for instance) or colluding with select private entities (large corporations) to control resources and wealth and preserve the private usurious credit system.

The invention of credit and its widespread application in the early modern era was a promising revolution gone very awry. The new credit could have played the role of a new commons, but it did not. Credit, rather than land or resources or wealth, could have been used to reestablish an equitable claim to resources by all members of the community. What a system of public credit could have done—and still could do—is give to any able-bodied person capable of productive activity access to a fair share of money, as a line of credit, on good collateral so they can invest in themselves and their families. But this must be non-usurious credit, for only by the elimination of usurious interest can we ensure that the benefits of any loans go to the borrower, and, through a multitude of borrowers, to society itself. This approach, as we shall see in chapter seven, involves no taking of assets from anyone; it instead distributes credit to all productive citizens.

Reformers today sometimes call for public credit to replace private credit, for federal spending in the United States, for instance, to supplement and perhaps replace Wall Street investment. But a government-run financial system, we should not forget, can be just as usurious as a privatized one. And even a non-usurious system, if credit continues to be issued in a centralized, top-down manner, will create a elite distributing and controlling resources as they see fit. The best way of ensuring fair and full access to a new commons of credit is to ensure fair and full access to credit without usury, and on a decentralized, personalized basis. The essence of the financial revolution—the shift from money as a commodity to money as debt—turned money into a futures claim on resources. This was in itself a good thing. Debt money is a contractual obligation to be realized in the future; commodity money, by contrast, represents value already realized. *Instead of money having to be earned before it could be spent, it could now be spent before it had to be earned.* This ability to spend against the future instead of the past created a new and expansive claim against resources, that is, against the commons. Instead of making resources in kind (fields, forests, fisheries, etc.) available to communities on a case by case basis, as the old commons did, any desired resource could now be obtained by anyone with access to money, which now included a large and growing group of people with the ability to borrow. The challenge is to ensure that such access to non-usurious credit is fairly made available to all.

All resources in these circumstances become potentially available to all through the common medium of debt. If a token or debt currency—in contrast to a non-debt, commodity currency—can be made available to anyone on loans with good collateral *without* the onerous burden of usurious interest rates or centralized financial authority, then viable and fair access to the commons, that is, to the common wealth available at any time in the marketplace, can be reestablished. This new commons would be not a pasture or woodlot or some particular material thing, but rather the ability to command through credit one's fair share of the entire range of community resources, as available on the market, at one's discretion. Insofar as anyone with good collateral can access capital without usury, then capital can be steadily and fairly distributed to those willing and able to use it. Unearned income, of the sort taken at the expense of debtors by creditors, would become a thing of the past. The wealth already in possession of individuals, no matter how obtained, would not be confiscated; but it would no longer be a source of unearned income. It would either be spent, or, if it is to be maintained, invested in productive activities. [20]

NOTES

1. Henry Roseveare, *The Financial Revolution 1660–1760* (London: Longman, 1991), p. 14.

2. Pierre Vilar, *A History of Gold and Money: 1450–1920*, Judith White, trans. (New York: Verso, 1976), p. 206.

3. Ibid., p. 207.

4. Niall Ferguson, *The Ascent of Money* (New York: Penguin, 2008), p. 49.

5. Henry Roseveare, *The Financial Revolution 1660–1760* (London, Longman, 1991), p. 37.

6. Hollis, *The Two Nations*, (New York: Gordon Press, 1975), pp. 29–30.

7. P. G. M. Dickson, *The Financial Revolution in England* (London: Macmillan, 1967), p. 457.

8. John Brewer, *The Sinews of Power* (Cambridge: Harvard University Press, 1990), p. 10.

9. Ibid., p. 27.

10. Ibid., p. 42.

11. Ibid., pp. 186–7.

12. P. G. M. Dickson, *The Financial Revolution in England* (London: Macmillan, 1967), pp. 257, 265, 292, 295, 436, 464

13. Glyn Davies, *A History of Money From Ancient Times to the Present Day* (Cardiff: University of Wales Press, 2002), p. 281.

14. Ibid., p. 282.

15. John Brewer, *The Sinews of Power* (Cambridge: Harvard University Press, 1990), p. 204.

16. David Armitage, "'The Projecting Age': William Paterson and the Bank of England." (*History Today*. 44.6, 1994, pp. 5–10), Platinum Periodicals, ProQuest. Web. Nov. 2009, p. 1

17. Ibid., p. 3.

18. Cf. Carlo M. Cipolla, *Before the Industrial Revolution: European Society and Economy, 1000–1700* (New York: W. W. Norton, 1976), pp. 211–13.

19. Cf. T. S. Ashton, *The Industrial Revolution 1760–1830* (London, Oxford University Press, 1968) pp.18–9.

20. For an earlier discussion of this issue, see Adrian Kuzminski, *Fixing the System: A History of Populism, Ancient & Modern* (New York: Continuum, 2008), pp. 131–148.

Chapter Five

The Industrial Revolution

I propose to show in this chapter how the widespread practice of usurious credit, which lay at the heart of the financial revolution of the seventeenth and eighteenth centuries, was indispensable to the industrial revolution, the opening act of the modern economy and of modernity itself. This is to explain one revolution by another: an industrial revolution by a financial revolution. Much has been written about the causes of the industrial revolution, yet to this day they are poorly understood. Industrialization was made possible in physical terms, above all, by the exploitation of fossil fuels with their incredible potency which, for the first time, made powerful machinery feasible. Some commentators have presumed the physical discovery of such fuels, beginning with coal, to be a sufficient explanation for industrial development. But the ready availability of a resource does not translate automatically into its serious use. Even though the energy potential of wood had been recognized since prehistoric times, for instance, and the technology for its intensive exploitation (first manifest in the steam engine) was developed in antiquity, wood was never exploited, as it might have been, to power industrial scale machinery before the eighteenth century, except in a few isolated cases, such as ceramics and metallurgy.

Other causal hypotheses remain debatable as well. The political stability of Britain, home of the industrial revolution, its relative security from invasion, the early dismantling of feudal structures in that country, and the early relative commercialization of its economy, have all been cited as providing an essential context for a new kind of industrial production. Yet a stable political and social context, a relative lack of feudal institutions, and even widespread commercialization, do not in themselves explain the pervasive impetus towards industrialization first manifest in Britain in the eighteenth century. Similar conditions existed at times in antiquity (in Greece, Rome,

China, and elsewhere) without sparking an industrial revolution. Debate about these and other factors has become ever more complex and inconclusive. As a result, the development of agriculture and industry has come to be broadly regarded by historians as multi-factorial in origin, resistant to any singular explanation. Overarching historical explanations, once popular with Marxists, Freudians, and others, have fallen out of fashion.

Most historians today remain hesitant to draw conclusions. But cautious generalizations are still sometimes advanced. One prominent older historian of the subject, David S. Landes, writes

> if I had to single out the critical, distinctively European sources of success [in achieving an industrial revolution] I would emphasize three considerations: (1) the growing *autonomy* of intellectual inquiry; (2) the development of unity in disunity in the form of a common, implicitly adversarial *method*, that is, the creation of a language of proof recognized, used, and understood across national and cultural boundaries; and (3) the invention of invention, that is, the *routinization* of research and its diffusion.[1]
> (author's emphasis)

Landes sees the industrial revolution as the climax of an incremental process in which a variety of factors gradually develop and interact until they reach a critical, synergistic threshold: a new and compelling whole somehow arises out of what were a series of disparate parts. These parts include the factors usually cited: a stable political and legal framework, a tolerant, reasonably open culture, a commercialized economy, and a tradition of science and technical innovation. What is not clear is why this brew should have ignited an unprecedented transformation of human life on earth. This can only be explained, I shall argue, by making explicit a largely overlooked synthesizing and enabling factor: the new and revolutionary financial system described in the last chapter which was established in Britain by the early the eighteenth century.

Traditional inquiry into the causes of the industrial revolution recognizes, but minimizes, a role for finance. Contemporary financial historians continue to display a characteristic ambivalence. Niall Ferguson puts it this way:

> Financial historians disagree as to how far the growth of banking after the seventeenth century can be credited with the acceleration of economic growth that began in Britain. . . . It may in fact be futile to seek a simplistic causal relationship (more sophisticated financial institutions caused growth or growth spurred on financial development). It seems perfectly plausible that the two processes were interdependent and self-reinforcing.[2]

The central thesis of this book is that "more sophisticated financial institutions" did indeed "cause growth," that in fact the rehabilitation and institutionalization of the previously illegal practice of usury unleashed the financial revolution, which in turn unleashed the industrial revolution and the endless growth that has come in its wake. What Landes, Ferguson and other writers miss is the catalyst which ignited the industrial revolution and modernity: the establishment of a broad but usurious credit market backed by state debt for the first time in Britain by the early eighteenth century. My hypothesis is that interest-bearing credit not only made the industrial revolution possible, but literally commanded it into being. Indeed, its role turns out to have been central not only to the industrial revolution but to the entire economics of growth which came to underlie the modern world.

The idea that interest-bearing credit is the key to the industrial revolution helps explain why it did not happen earlier, especially in the Roman era, or perhaps in China. Chinese commerce and invention—particularly in the Sung and Ming eras—was legendary, but no industrial revolution followed. In ancient Rome as in China we see many of the preconditions for an industrial revolution. In both places a high level of monetization and commerce developed, as it did later in early modern Europe, along with a considerable use of credit, including usury; there were major engineering feats (roads, aqueducts, canals, public buildings) and even factories (mass producing weapons and some consumer goods), but yet no industrial revolution occurred. Why did an industrial revolution not take off in the Roman era? One inhibiting factor—also found in China—was that the commercial development of the ancient world was relatively centralized. Rather than a plethora of competing cities and states as in the early modern European West, the rise of Rome after the defeat of Carthage was largely the story of one city-state and of its ruling elites becoming dominant. The earlier commercial successes of Phoenicians and Greeks were achieved by a number of independent and comparatively decentralized and competing city-states, but these were eventually swallowed by monolithic Hellenistic kingdoms, and finally by Rome. The focusing of great wealth in one ruling city may help account for the stalling of commercial activity, albeit at a high level.

Further, commerce in Rome (or China) never shed its second-class status. The Chinese Mandarins eschewed commerce. Roman senators were forbidden to engage in commercial ventures, which were left to the second class of knights, who remained politically disadvantaged in spite of their wealth. Even though these social rules were sometimes circumvented, motivation for innovation in commerce and credit was thereby not as compelling as it might otherwise have been. The highest social values were not pecuniary, but rather those of civic virtue and personal dignity – much as found in classical China, where political power was also highly centralized and a bureaucratic elite of Mandarins reinforced a conservative status quo. There was also but limited wage-labor in the ancient world and extensive slavery, and only a minimal development of what came to be known in modern times as joint-stock companies. There were financial booms and panics in Rome, to be sure, and

shares in public corporations (mostly tax farming operations) were specula-
tively traded (though not in an organized stock market), but this reflected
only a small percentage of Roman wealth.

Putting all these factors aside, however, perhaps the most significant difference, by comparison with the modern era, is that credit remained personalized and marginal to the overall economy. Rich men borrowed from one
another, even at usurious rates, but the Roman state itself —like the Chinese
state—rarely borrowed money and had no ongoing national debt.[3] The lack
of a mature credit system kept the Roman economy in an economic straight-
jacket. As one classic economic historian of Rome put it:

> the incessant taxation required to pay for the mercenary troops enrolled and to
> feed, clothe, and arm the troops, must be reckoned as one of the chief factors
> in the destruction of imperial resources. Had it been possible to spread the
> costs of such sudden wars over a period of years, as is now done by means of
> national loans, the consequences need not have been so serious.[4]

The taxing power of the Roman state was never harnessed to underwrite a
credit system. And without a institutionalized credit system, the Roman
economy (like China's)—impressive as it was in scale—remain stalled and
exposed to disruption.

The ancient world may have come to the threshold of the industrial revolution technologically, but it did not cross the line which was finally passed
only in the eighteenth century in Britain. Perhaps more tellingly, Rome did
not even achieve a full-blown commercial economy—a precondition for an
industrial revolution—though it did develop large-scale commercial activities. What distinguishes a full-blown commercial economy is the use of
credit for transactions in place of direct purchase. As we have seen, I can go
to market with gold coins and buy goods and services, but this kind of direct
exchange can support no more than a steady-state economy since I must be
ready to hand over in advance the full value (in coin) for my purchase. Credit
in such a situation has not yet replaced commodity currencies. Even ordinary
people, such as small farmers or freeholders, could and did borrow money in
ancient times, sometimes at usurious rates, but since money had to be borrowed only from someone who already had it (unlike our system, where it is
borrowed from institutions which invent it), and since usury continued to be
discouraged, the scope of credit vis-à-vis the larger economy remained limited. No doubt some forms of bills of credit were in use in ancient times—
otherwise long distance trade is hard to imagine—but somehow they never
became central to the overall economy.

The key idea that credit could be used to *create* money was not yet
grasped. The financial revolution of the seventeenth and eighteenth centuries
in Europe not only made credit much more widely available, but transformed

credit into an instrument of money creation. By institutionalizing the free invention of credit, a new kind of financial system and a new kind of money was created. Since credit allows me to defer payment while spending money, it allows for investment not otherwise possible, and therefore for production which would not otherwise occur. It allows us to draw against the future, not merely the present. But if credit is made widely available only on usurious terms, as turned out to be the case in early modern Europe beginning with Britain, then additional production is not only possible, but necessary.

For credit to become dominant in commercial arrangements it needs what the Romans never provided: the backing of the state, that is, the willingness of the state to guarantee not only the stability of its currency, but also to provide some kind of security for loans made with it—generally through taxes—even when more money was loaned than actually existed. This, as we shall see, is what the "monied men" managed to achieve in Britain at the end of the seventeenth century, following in the footsteps of the Dutch. They realized something missed even by the Dutch: that not only could they leverage debt by loaning out more than they held in reserve, but that they could entrain the force of the state to guarantee such loans for their private benefit. They did it by transforming the personal debt of the monarch into a national debt held by wealthy elites backed by the taxing power of the state. And, in a profound historical twist, they tacked on usury as a condition of most loans. Once usurious debt was backed by the tax revenues of the state, not only was debt made respectable: it was able to dominate economic life.

To return to the industrial revolution, historians of the subject have pointed to a variety of causal factors to account for its specific beginnings in Britain. An extended list would include the early use of coal in that country, a stable political system, developed property rights, a concentration of capital through commercial activities centered on London (including the slave trade), the scientific revolution and associated technical innovations, the role of religious dissenters (Quakers and others), among others. The role of credit (including money and banking) is usually listed as one among these many factors, but it is not given a central, let alone the major, role. The growth of credit, before it blossomed forth in the seventeenth century, was a long and slow process, as we have seen. It took hundreds of years to move from medieval oral agreements and personal oaths as the essence of contracts to written forms, and then for written contracts (especially bills of exchange) to be widely and impersonally negotiable.[5] The weakening and eventual overturning of prohibitions against usury was also a gradual process, and the usurious nature of this new credit is generally downplayed in modern historical accounts.[6] Yet credit, once made usurious and broadly available, can be understood as the most decisive factor in unleashing the industrial revolution. And this is precisely what occurred at the turn of the seventeenth century in Britain.

Let us examine this process in more detail. Embedded in the work of various historians are key passages, often made in passing, which elucidate this process. The following passage from a classic work on the subject, T. S. Ashton's *The Industrial Revolution, 1760-1830*, lays out the role of credit in the industrial revolution, as enabled by the new banking system. It is worth quoting at length:

> The chief contribution of the banks to the industrial revolution consisted in the mobilizing of short-term funds and their transfer from areas where there was little demand for them to others that were hungry for capital. In the agricultural counties landlords, farmers, and dealers paid in to the local banks the bills and cash they received as rent or payment for produce (they were paid interest on the sum deposited or were given interest-bearing notes). The banks remitted the bills to their correspondent bank in London which, after collecting them, found itself with considerable funds. These it used to discount bills for banks in industrial centres, which were thus in turn able to lend to their clients currency, in the form of drafts or bills on London, or cash. The movement took place mainly in the late autumn and early winter, when the crops were being sold; but this was the very time when the manufacturers, who settled their accounts at the end of the year, were most in need of funds. The marriage between the thrift of the South and East and the enterprise of the Midlands and the North was both happy and fertile. It meant in effect that rural England was providing foodstuffs for the growing urban communities without requiring an immediate return, and that industrial England was thus able to use its own resources to put up factories and construct canals and railways which benefited manufacturing and agricultural areas alike. [7]

Consider in addition to this the confirming testimony of another financial historian of the era, Leland Jenks:

> In the agricultural areas of southeast England, in Norfolk and Suffolk, and in Somersetshire, bankers accumulated deposits which they did not see their way to lay out locally to advantage. Notes had replaced specie in their local trade, and the accessibility of London by mail-coach after 1784 made it convenient to carry their reserves there for more remote banks. At the same time, the resources of banks in Lancashire and Yorkshire were continually strained by the demands of their local merchants and manufacturers for loans. [8]

It was still relatively difficult in the eighteenth century, in spite of this growing credit system, to raise capital for long-term investment, and historians have debated to what extent the British banking system directly funded industrial development.[9] The consensus of recent historians, as Ashton and Jenks represent it, is that banking was crucial in providing short-term credit to manufacturers, and less of a factor, though still an important one, in securing longer term credit. Relatively low start-up costs for early factories and financing through family connections and partnerships were alternatives which meant less reliance on the banks. But it is misleading to focus narrowly on direct lending by banks. The important thing is that credit, via the newly institutionalized financial system, had become an indispensable factor in more and more productive enterprises, whether in agricultural or manufacturing. And the important thing about this credit—wherever it came from—was its usurious nature. A steady-state traditional economy was no longer good enough. It was now necessary to grow, not just for a time, but continually. A steady-state economy can grow arithmetically (given a discovery here, an invention there) but its essential reciprocity forces a return to a baseline where inputs and outputs have to be balanced. A growth economy by contrast grows geometrically without any return to baseline. The natural balance of inputs and outputs is disrupted. The producer working with money borrowed at usurious rates *must* consistently come up with more outputs than inputs to cover his costs, and that total must be something beyond the natural replacement rate of a reciprocal, steady-state economy.

The Bank of England played a crucial role not so much as a lender but as a financial backstop for lending in general. Unlike earlier banks, as we have seen, it was able to rely upon the taxing revenue of the state to back its bonds. This was the final revolutionary innovation—the last essential component of the modern financial complex—and particularly once the national debt became permanent. It allowed, for the first time, a stable credit market which in effect underwrote all other financial markets. The interest charged on government bonds issued by the bank set a standard for interest rates—something hitherto lacking. *Since anyone could buy the bonds, and get the going rate for their money, a benchmark level of expectation was set for all lending.* What mattered was not so much how much lending banks or anyone else did, but the fact that all lending, including private credit, was now effectively based upon the going, usurious interest rate institutionalized in government bonds more or less continually available to the public. The ultimate symbol of this system was the British consol, a consolidated perpetual annuity (hence the name) first offered by the government at 3.5 percent in 1752 (and still available today).

Britain, with an important assist from Holland, was the first of the major powers of Europe (or anywhere) to develop a credit system able to operate on a national scale not only to finance the government and central sectors of the economy, but to provide a uniform standard of credit. Only in those countries was credit available in more or less open markets (especially bond markets) in relatively large quantities. The advantages of this new credit, albeit it usurious, allowed Britain to fund forces sufficient to defeat its main global competitor in the eighteenth century: the much larger but cash-strapped, credit-starved, semi-feudal French monarchy. And whereas large-scale finance earlier had been confined mainly to individual transactions among monarchs and elites, the new usurious credit system percolated through impersonal institutions and instruments down to the local level, especially once ordinary people got used to depositing savings in banks. Another historian of the industrial revolution, Peter Mathias, puts the point as follows:

> The banker's role as a professional intermediary, standing between the savings of those receiving surpluses and those needing credit, could be as important within a locality as with such national flows. Such an institutional develop- ment meant that the inadequacies of depending on personal, face-to-face con- tacts to equate saving and borrowing were being overcome, so that savings ceased to be largely hoarded, sterilized from productive use, and became acti- vated, if only because bankers had to make greater profits by using the funds which their customers deposited with them than the interest they had to pay on these deposits themselves. [10]

The last sentence is crucial. Instead of money largely ending up in mattress- es, so to speak, as in most pre-industrial societies, it was now "activated." No longer was it necessary to be a miser or hoarder to protect your assets; you could now put your money safely to work through legally protected invest- ments and institutions, underwritten ultimately by taxpayer-funded govern- ment debt, and watch it "grow" magically. *The bulk of national savings for the first time passed into the financial system, which immediately put it to use.* Not only could it be lent out to someone else; it could repeatedly be lent out. What had been numerous but discreet individual transactions in pre- modern societies, became part of an integrated and continuous process. The goldsmiths of London, as we have seen, had discovered in the mid-seven- teenth century a very potent way of activating money: fractional reserve banking. Only a small part of the gold put on deposit with them, they real- ized, would normally be withdrawn at any one time. The remainder they could confidently lend out or otherwise invest. When fractional reserve bank- ing as the basis of lending was combined with the idea of a national central bank, as occurred with the Bank of England in 1694, the result was a unprec- edented compounding of the money supply. Leland Jenks puts the outcome this way: "The age of . . . baroque, of flamboyant fashion, of elaborate speech, could not be accused of miserliness. Nor would the candid historian insist that it was industrious. Yet under the fermenting influence of the newly discovered note and deposit system the capital resources of Great Britain grew by leaps and bounds during the closing decades of the century." [11]

The initial motive for this activation, for securing and expanding the money supply and putting money to work, was the need of bankers to get a greater rate of return by lending out the assets of their depositors than the rate of interest they offered those same depositors. The money which circulated in earlier times was almost always commodity money, as we've noted, either coins minted by the sovereign, or occasionally some other token of real wealth (such as tally sticks in England, or wampum in early America). Most traditional monies were inactive (not yet 'activated'); they served mostly passively as repositories of value and media of exchange for what, compared to later industrial times, was a modest scale of commercial activity (trade in luxuries, textiles, and other artisanal goods, and a few basic commodities like grain, salt, etc.). The supply of money before the financial revolution was relatively inelastic (there being only so many precious metals, or other suitable materials of intrinsic value), but relatively speaking not much money was needed. The medieval tradition of usury laws helped ensure monetary inelasticity. What expansion there was of the money supply was due mainly to accidental discoveries of gold and silver in the New World. Although these new precious metals acted as a stimulus to economic activity, such expansion still remained limited by the actual supply available. The new usurious credit system, by contrast, was able to create a flood of money through lending not on the basis of more or less objective and static current assets but on the basis of more or less subjective and dynamic prospects for future wealth. It became possible, for the first time, to divorce money from reality. Value was subtle shifted away from real things existing now, to someone's promise to produce such things in the future. It was a triumph of the imagination.

In Britain by the eighteenth century we see the first large nation-state economy beginning to run on usurious credit, rather than on land and the reciprocity of a traditional economy, that is, an economy no longer content to run on subsistence, or renewable resources, but increasingly subject to imperatives pushing beyond them: including, above all, legal contracts committing debtors to pay back significantly more than they borrowed. This breakout from the constraints of traditional economics is key to the rise of British power in the modern world, which in turn set the pattern for the United States, Britain's successor as world super-power. Britain's main rival France, then the largest economy in Europe, remained hampered by the persistence of medieval practices in the *ancien regime* which favored the continuation of a land-based economy of renewable but limited resources. Eighteenth century French physiocrats still saw land and traditional reciprocal exchange as the source of all wealth. They were right, thinking in terms of sustainability, as they did implicitly; what they did not appreciate was the ability of humans to fashion practices that violate sustainability.

The British credit system institutionalized the rate of interest, and attached it like an incubus onto the body of credit. Credit plus interest was no longer bound in this new system by the limits of established procedures of production through renewable resources, but rather by a new master: by the returns demanded by the going rate of interest, most manifest when it is compounded (reinvested). It is one thing for credit to be available against the future; it is quite another to condition such credit on the payment of an extra charge, or usury. In spite of an extended rear-guard action by some in opposition to the reintroduction of usury,[12] there was remarkably little understanding and consequently little protest against the profound transformation wrought by the institutionalization of usurious interest on loans.[13] And today, of course, the charging of interest on loans is almost always taken for granted. The old sustainable subsistence economy was an economy of exchange and reciprocity. Gains and losses balanced out one another—high birth and death rates, renewable resources used renewably—leaving little room for growth. The new "growth" economy broke all the old rules.

Once the British economy was restructured into a credit economy from an exchange economy, the stage was set for profound transformation. The new financial system, if this analysis is correct, based on usurious credit unleashed the industrial revolution, and the long subsequent binge of economic "growth," now well over two hundred years running. Investors, that is, creditors, came to play the dominant role in sectors across the economy, from nascent manufacturing to agriculture, all through the credit instruments and institutions created in the financial revolution: fractional reserve banking, a central bank, joint-stock companies, a national debt, perpetual securities, bills of exchange, mortgages, bonds, a money market, a stock market, etc. This full ensemble of ingredients was unprecedented. Capital was suddenly much more available, but, again, *only on condition of usurious rates of interest*. The result was a steady ratcheting up of economic activity. Early industrialists, like most borrowers since, had to commit themselves to being able to *increase* their production to come out ahead. The steady-state economics of the pre-industrial era was over; the new rule was grow or die.

With the new usurious credit economy came the booms and busts so familiar in modern history, since credit tended to get overextended until debtors defaulted, with default being the only long-run check on credit. Overextended credit creates bubbles, where liabilities, unbeknownst to investors, exceed assets. John Law's famous Mississippi bubble in France was based on a deal by which shares of the Mississippi Company he headed would be backed by government debt—an attempt (unsuccessful) by Law to implement a version of "the English System" in France. In a few months from 1719 to early 1720 shares in the Mississippi Company rose from 500 to 18,000 livres, before collapsing later that year, losing almost all of their value. The result was an unprecedented crisis which destroyed the embryonic French financial system, along with Law's reputation. While the contemporaneous South Sea bubble in Britain also precipitated a financial crisis, the more resilient financial institutions in that country weathered the storm and allowed for a recovery and a subsequent re-expansion of the for-profit credit system. In France, however, recovery was limited to the traditional agricultural and trade patterns; the credit boosts which continued in Britain led to a kind of growth not found subsequently in France, or any other traditional society, and given the underlying bankruptcy of the French monarchy, compounded by a series of disasters in the course of the eighteenth century, especially its defeat in the Seven Years War, the stage was set for the Revolution of 1789.

While eighteenth century Britain managed to reinflate its credit system after the crash of South Sea shares and to go on to stimulate enough economic growth to support an expanding supply of credit, a pattern often since repeated, such options may no longer be available today, in the wake of the great crash of 2008. It appears we face not simply a cyclical recession, but a fundamental financial, commercial, and perhaps eventual political long-term downsizing, with little prospect of recovery to old levels given global resource depletion and the ecological limits constraining real economic growth. One silver lining to such a retrenchment—call it the end of the industrial revolution—would be the opportunity it presents to reinvent the financial, economic, and political system. This would mean a chance at establishing a financial framework for a sustainable society, one which avoids the abuses of usurious credit and forced exponential growth. If usurious lending has been instrumental in driving the exponential growth of the modern industrial economy over the last two hundred and fifty years or so, a key step toward sustainability would be to abolish it. But usurious credit is central to modern societies; to abolish it would be to abolish, to a large extent, those very societies themselves.

The industrial economy as we know it, if I am right, is a usurious economy. If it were not for the mutual commitment of creditor and debtor to conspire to attempt to extract *a continual excess* over current return on assets for their anticipated mutual benefit, we would not be driven to over-exploit our resources, let alone to push beyond their carrying capacity. Usurious credit makes the expectation of an excess over current return more or less permanent. The wealth of nations, by contrast, if no longer hitched to innumerable binding contracts mediated by centralizing institutions and rooted in expectations of growth, would be able to reflect more realistically the facts of physics, biology, and ecology, where unlimited growth is not the norm but a fatal aberration. The explosion of wealth by the exploitation of nonrenewable resources by the industrialized nations has made nearly everyone in the short term much richer in terms of goods and services, compared with the limited wealth available to societies constrained by renewable resources. But enjoyment of this relative wealth has been conditioned not only on debt servitude—essentially forced labor on behalf of a very small number of creditors whose power and influence is almost beyond imagination—but also on using up the natural and renewable capital of the earth. We are in debt peonage to the earth as well as to our creditors, and the day of reckoning is upon us.

This is the seamy underside story of our industrial revolution, with its familiar "growth" dynamic: unsustainable levels of debt driven by a usurious financial system. We can no longer afford it, by many indications, either financially or ecologically. There is simply no way, it seems, for economic productivity—that is, actual production and services—to increase so as to match the increase in debt levels, even as it is spurred to do so by those very debt levels. Here, in another context, we see the same contrast drawn by Malthus with regard to population and resources. In our case, the contrast of arithmetic vs. exponential increases he drew for populations reappears with regard to resources on the one hand and debt on the other. As exponentially increasing debt levels outstrip any possibility of eventual repayment, lenders and debtors struggle to avoid defaults, by taking on even more debt, cutting expenses, and finally by selling out in an attempt to recover what they can, if they survive. The financial crash, like the crash of overpopulation, is likely to come suddenly and decisively when it finally comes. In the many examples of finite resources trying to support exponential growth, the crisis comes only at the very end. The algae in a nutrient rich pond grow quickly, but they finally overcrowd the pond and die-off only on the last day of their accelerating expansion. On the next-to-last day, there still seems to be plenty of room, for at that point the pond is only half full of algae.

NOTES

1. David S. Landes, *The Wealth and Poverty of Nations: Why some are so Rich and some so Poor* (New York: W. W. Norton, 1999), p. 201.

2. Niall Ferguson, *The Ascent of Money* (New York: Penguin, 2008), pp. 52–3.

3. Cf. Scott B. MacDonald and Albert L. Gastmann, *A History of Credit and Power in the Western World* (New Brunswick: Transaction Publishers, 2001), p. 9.

4. Tenny Frank, *An Economic History of Rome* [1920] (New York: Cosimo Classics, 2005), p. 487.

5. The long history of the evolution of credit in Europe before the modern era is given in detail in Abbott Payson Usher's *The Early History of Deposit Banking in Mediterranean Europe*, 2 vols. (Cambridge: Harvard University Press, 1943).

6. See for example, recent works by Niall Ferguson: *The Cash Nexus: Money and Power in the Modern World 1700–2000* (New York: Basic Books, 2001), and *The Ascent of Money: A Financial History of the World* (New York: Penguin Press, 2008); Ferguson's generally celebratory account of modern finance glosses over usury prohibitions as a "taboo" to be overcome (*The Ascent of Money*, p. 35) .

7. T. S. Ashton, *The Industrial Revolution: 1760-1830* (London, Oxford University Press, 1968). p. 74.

8. Leland H. Jenks, *The Migration of British Capital to 1875* (New York, Harper & Row, 1973), p. 21.

9. See Michael Collins, *Banks and Industrial Finance in Britain 1800-1939* (Cambridge: Cambridge University Press, 1991), *et passim*.

10. Peter Mathias, *The First Industrial Nation: An Economic History of Britain 1700–1914* (London: Methuen, 1983, 2nd ed.), p. 134.

11. Jenks, *Migration of British Capital*, p. 9.

12. Cf. for one example, Wilson, Thomas, *A Discourse Upon Usury, by Way of Dialogue and Orations, for the Better Variety and More Delight of All Those that Shall Read this Treatise* [1572], Introduction by R. H. Tawney. (New York: Augustus M. Kelley, 1963), et passim; see also the strange case of Father Jeremiah O'Callaghan, recounted by Benjamin Nelson in his *The Idea of Usury: From Tribal Brotherhood to Universal Otherhood* (Chicago: University of Chicago Press, 1969), pp. 124–132.

13. Jeremy Bentham's "Defense of Usury" [1816] in *The Works of Jeremy Bentham*, published under the superintendence of his executor, John Bowring, vol. 3, (New York: Russell & Russell, 1962), seems to have been the last mainstream rebuttal to the lingering critique of usury.

Chapter Six

Natural and Unnatural Interest

Usury is central to our story. It distorts credit by artificially magnifying the gains and losses imposed by the financial system. Let us examine this dynamic in more detail. Credit in itself, we should not forget, is a very good thing without which much that is valuable would not be accomplished, but its danger increases directly in proportion as interest rates rise. A few percent interest on a loan may not seem like an intolerable circumstance, and indeed it is not for small sums taken out of a large cash flow. In an expanding economy affordability is even less of a burden, as future increases in wealth can be expected to absorb high interest costs in stride. Yet as anyone who has taken on a large debt in proportion to income and assets, such as a mortgage, an auto loan, a student loan, or a large credit card balance, can testify, the multiplier effect is enormous and potentially devastating. An accounting principle, the rule of 72—sometimes called the investment rule, or the compound interest rule of 72—is a useful illustration of the debt burden. It provides us with an important rule of thumb for assessing the risk burden. If you divide 72 by the interest rate, you get the time it takes for the principle on a loan to equal the interest paid out, that is, the time it takes to double the principle at any given rate of interest. This is a practical measure of the burden of interest on borrowers, individually and collectively, as well as of the return accrued to lenders.

If money is lent out at one percent a year interest, for instance, it will take 72 years for the interest to equal the principle of that investment, that is, a lifetime. At two percent, it takes 36 years; at three percent, 24 years; at four percent, 18 years; at five percent, 14.4 years; at six percent, 12 years; at seven percent, 10.3 years; and so on. At ten percent, it takes only 7.2 years; at fifteen percent, 4.8 years; at twenty percent, 3.6 years; and so on at ever accelerating rates. The more rapidly one can use and pay back borrowed money, the less the burden. Most people who borrow money cannot repay it quickly; they often refinance, and so end up for much if not most of their lives continually in debt. Since mortgages make up the largest sector of the traditional debt market, and are one of the most widely familiar forms of debt, we can take them as illustrative of modern credit norms. In recent decades mortgage rates have fluctuated around 5 to 6 percent annually— sometimes much higher and recently lower. A homeowner borrowing at 5 percent will end up paying back twice what he or she borrowed in less than 15 years. Even with the artificially low interest rates following the 2008 crash, most mortgages are still around 4 percent. Since debts in the modern economy are not eliminated, but constantly renewed, the debt burden for society as a whole, rather than for an individual, is for all practical purposes never-ending.

Let us consider the economy as a whole as if it were a perpetual household with a perpetual debt burden, and imagine a perpetual debt to be one which is continually refinanced. As we pay down our principal with interest on one loan, we take out a second loan, thus maintaining an ongoing state of indebtedness. In society as a whole individual debtors come and go, one loan is paid off and another taken out, so that the overall debt level continues. If our "household" (that is, society) carries $100,000 in debt perpetually at one percent a year, it will take us 72 years of interest payments for the total interest paid to be equal to the principal, that is, to $100,000; it will take another 72 years—for a total of 144 years—to pay twice the interest, or $200,000; and so on. A one percent interest rate is a relatively light burden. It amounts to having 72 years to earn enough to pay the interest before the interest equals the principal. So far so good. But at higher interest rates we are compelled to work increasingly harder. At two percent, as we have seen, we have only 34 years before the interest mounts up to equal the principal; there is less and less time allowed as rates go up. At six percent we have only 12 years before our interest obligation matches our obligation for the principal. To pay the interest at whatever rate is set, we must produce and sell goods and services at a comparable rate. The higher the interest the more we must produce and sell, at a exponentially increasing rate. All this additional expense is above and beyond satisfying our own needs; it does us no good whatsoever. Instead it goes to someone else, to our creditor. It constitutes a debt burden which can be so heavy as to end in debt peonage, a situation of perpetual debt where the interest is so high as to impoverish the borrower and to render final repayment impossible for all practical purposes.

This interest doesn't go to the community, but to its creditors. In a self-contained community they would be just one part of the community, and usually a small part. It's true that creditors reinvest—that is, reloan—most of the money, but only on the condition of receiving more interest, thus maintaining borrowers perpetually as clients, like indentured servants. The rule of

72 is a dramatic illustration of the dynamic of usury working to the advantage of the creditor at the expense of the debtor, and of its power to transfer wealth from one party to another, and to concentrate it in few hands rather than disperse it among many. Critics of usury down the centuries have focused on this very real injustice. I wish to bring an additional indictment against usury, one equally if not more devastating: its responsibility for the unsustainable exploitation of resources. The rule of 72 illustrates just how compelling and overwhelming the legal obligation to repay a debt can be, and precisely how much harder debtors must work to met that obligation, doing whatever it takes, including drawing down non-replaceable resources.

Modern money, it cannot be overstated, is almost entirely created by being loaned into existence, literally out of nothing, on somebody's legally authorized say so, to individuals and corporations, by a private financial system centered on the commercial banks, which exercises this magic for its own profit. But there is nothing magical about the repayment of loans; that must be done the hard way, through labor and production. Most modern economists downplay not only the role of interest but even credit itself, and talk instead of supply and demand, confidence, productivity, "free markets," labor costs, and other factors. As a result, the burden of usury has been obscured. The idea that money is created by issuing debt is largely ignored, especially by those who understand what is going on and who perhaps prefer to let sleeping dogs lie; at the same time, repayment remains a conspicuous public duty, a universal law. Since the crash of 2008 there has been heightened criticism of the excesses of the financial and monetary system, and as a result the evils of usurious lending have again been dramatized, but so far no serious attempt at fundamental reform has been made. The privatized usurious monetary system remains firmly fixed in place, and largely unquestioned.

One recent exception to this conspiracy of silence over the real role of credit is William F. Hixon, whose principal work *A Matter of Interest: Reexamining Money, Debt, and Real Economic Growth*, was published in 1991.[1] Hixon points out that traditional economists have perpetuated the myth that savings are the source of investment. The perpetuation of this belief not only obscures the debt nature of modern token money, he argues, but it disguises interest and usury, making them seem far more benign than they are. He deconstructs this myth, quite succinctly, as follows:

> Suppose, for example, a manufacturer produces an item for which he pays out $100 in wages and other costs. In order to obtain a profit of $20 he establishes a selling price of $120. Only $100 in aggregate demand has been cast into circulation by the production process but $120 in circulation is required to assure the sale at a profit of $20. There thus arises a $20 insufficiency in demand. Expand the example to include all manufacturers in a large economy and there arises a large insufficiency in aggregate demand.[2]

In other words, as he goes on to add: ". . . in every time period there must be thrown into circulation not merely the costs of production of what is produced and marketed but the costs of new investments just equal to the profit markup on current production."[3] This is not money which has been saved because it has not yet been spent into existence.

If this extra new money to be thrown into circulation to keep the system going can't come from savings, where can it come from? The only remaining source is debt, but not debt created by borrowing from preexisting savings but debt created by creating money *which did not previously exist.* The myth of savings being the source of investment is a cover-up of this basic fact. This newly created debt is based not on current assets but on potential additional future assets which are expected to produce the extra $20 required in Hixon's example. In his words:

> the necessary increase in the money supply comes about by enterprises borrowing the newly created money—the previously nonexistent money—which private banking organizations create out of thin air through the operation of a system of fractional reserves, and the enterprises then spending for investment the new money thus created and borrowed. . . . The additional aggregate demand over and above production costs, the additional money supply that is required for the realization of profits, comes from introducing into circulation the newly created money (purchasing power) of banks.[4]

Hixon adds to this statement a supporting quotation from John Maynard Keynes: "If the grant of a bank-credit to an entrepreneur, additional to the credits already existing, allows him to make an addition to current investment which would not have occurred otherwise, incomes will necessarily be increased."

One more quote about the centrality of usurious debt from Hixon deserves to be pondered:

> That the economy is structured in such a way that growth and prosperity depend almost totally upon our going into debt to banks for the money they create is a fact of monumental importance to an understanding of how the economy works and why it sometimes does not work acceptably well. We are saddled with an economy structured in such a way as to make a crisis of over-indebtedness to banks an ever-present and ominous possibility. It is easily understandable why banks should want the economy structured in such a way that a tribute (in the form of interest on the checkbook money they create) would have to be paid to them by the rest of the economy for the right to grow and prosper. It is not so easy to understand why anyone else would want the economy structured in such a way or should be willing to tolerate it being so structured.[5]

It is impossible to overemphasize the importance of this "tribute" to modern "growth" economies. It is only the possibility of going into debt in the first place which allows us to imagine the growth and prosperity we think this debt will make possible for us. For it is only this debt which allows us access to resources not otherwise available. Only then are we able to think of what advantage we can derive from those resources once we can access them. Debt *per se* is not the culprit here. The culprit is *usurious* debt. A society unable to go into debt cannot make the necessary capital improvements to maintain a steady state, let alone a "growth," economy. Its economy will actually contract. A low-level or primitive subsistence economy can get by on little or no debt, but the infrastructure of a more complex subsistence society—including transportation, communications, housing, energy systems, and so on—requires large capital investment available generally only through debt, to be paid off over time, before having to be recapitalized in due course (as the infrastructure deteriorates) with more debt, and so on. Similarly an individual unable to go into debt cannot "invest" in himself or herself, cannot command the resources necessary to get an education, to buy a house, raise a family, and so on. Denied access to credit, and without some unusual windfall, he or she will gradually get poorer. Being able to borrow money to access capital is necessary to a healthy economy, personally as well as socially, *as long as natural capital is not depleted in the process, but replaced.* What forces us to borrow beyond the carrying capacity of our resources is not borrowing as such, but the requirement, imposed as a condition of borrowing, that loans be repaid at exponential or usurious rates of interest; this is the real "tribute" which is extracted.

Hixon makes the point theoretically that I have been trying to make historically: that credit has been essential to modern economic development. He also makes it clear that a monetary system based on commodity money could never raise what is needed for production out of savings. The lack of adequate credit was the fatal flaw of modern command societies, such as the Soviet Union. Credit is continuously needed to keep a modern economy going, *even at a steady state.* Ideally, this would be just enough to maintain the production necessary to replace what we consume, with innovation directed to efficiencies and sustainable practices. Prohibitions against usury, far from attacking interest as such, have traditionally been directed against excessive or unreasonable rates of interest, those beyond what the lender is thought to deserve. The effect of interest is to stimulate production. If no interest at all was charged, and only the principal were repaid, creditors would be made whole, and we would return to the *status quo ante* financially. *But the mere repayment of principal does not provide for the replacement of the resources the borrower has consumed using the borrowed money.* The economy in these circumstances would actually contract. In a usurious system, however, too much credit is not only provided but required, resulting not only in the unjust distribution of wealth and power but in overproduction, the excess exploitation of labor and resources, ending in economic overshoot. Historically there has been little to stop private creditors from imposing usurious interest rates, and we have traced the institutionalization of this practice culminating in "the English system" now dominant worldwide.

An example may be useful. Say I am able to put up enough collateral to borrow $100,000 interest free and I spend it to build a modest house. Without any interest to cover, I am obliged, no matter how long its takes, to go out and earn $100,000 to repay the principal, and no more; the wealth I create in doing so just equals the wealth I have borrowed and spent. Any more effort is voluntary, that is, not required by the loan. I may choose to earn more money to maintain and repair my house, but I could also let it deteriorate. On the other hand, if I were obliged to earn enough to compensate for the slow but inevitable depreciation of the value of the house, I would be have to go out and earn a second $100,000, that is, I would have to create, through my own further efforts, additional wealth equal to the value of my house, which would provide, in effect, for its replacement, or the equivalent thereof. If I had a one percent mortgage, as we saw in our discussion of the rule of 72, it would take me 72 years to meet that obligation. At higher and higher rates of interest, as we have seen, I would reach that point sooner and sooner.

The interest rate can be considered to be the mechanism by which additional production can be stimulated to earn enough income to compensate for a deteriorating resource such as a house. This is true of the economy as a whole. Insofar as modern economies are credit economies, and insofar as materials and labor, goods and services, must continuously be replenished as they are consumed or worn out, the interest rate serves as a spur to ensure the additional production needed to guarantee that replenishment. With no interest rate—a zero rate—production would tend to fall below replacement value. Of course, people and productive enterprises have many motives to produce, including a natural desire for improvement, opportunity for profit, intellectual curiosity, etc. But to eliminate interest on debt—a legally binding contractual obligation—would be to eliminate one of the most effective compulsions we have to replenish our labor and resources. In modern society, depending as it does on large and essential capital intensive systems which require significant debt (in manufacturing, transportation, communication, distribution, etc.), an absence of interest on debt would call into question our collective ability to maintain such systems.

Some interest, then, seems necessary to stability. The great difficulty is to determine how much. At what point does an interest rate become usurious? No answer offered to this long debated question has so far elicited enough support to resolve the debate. In this absence of consensus, let me propose the following definition: *A usurious rate of interest is one which, as far as society as a whole is concerned, depletes rather than replaces natural capi-*

tal. Natural capital is the totality of resources—physical and human—upon which we rely to produce goods and services for ourselves. Human beings, whose labor makes this process run, are just as much part of natural capital, are just as subject to being worn out, as the rest of the resources upon which the economy rests. They too must be continually replaced. *A non-usurious interest rate would be equivalent to the rate needed for a steady-state or replacement economy.* We might call this the *natural rate of interest*, or interest in compensation for the *natural rate of physical depreciation, or entropy.* If our goal is to replace rather than expand material resources, then we are thinking arithmetically, where things are added as they are subtracted; but if our goal is to expand those resources, we are thinking exponentially, not arithmetically. Today more than ever, we need a rate of interest calculated arithmetically, not exponentially. What would that rate be?

Like Goldilocks testing the porridge of the three bears, we need a rate of interest which is neither too cold (too low) nor too hot (too high and usurious) but just right. I submit that such a rate—approximating the replacement or depreciation rate in a non-growth or steady-state economy based on renewable resources—turns out to be about one percent, which is coincidentally, and revealingly, the approximate replacement rate for consumed resources over a lifetime. As we have seen, the interest on money borrowed at one percent will equal the principal in 72 years, roughly a human lifetime, or the productive part of it. This suggests that a one percent rate of interest is more or less equivalent to the sustainable replacement rate for society as a whole if we add together or aggregate all our individual lifetimes by applying a one percent rate across the board to all borrowing. "Man is the measure" applies in this case very nicely, for it captures what each of us owes to nature and society for our sustenance during our lives. In credit terms that means we ought to pay one percent—the natural rate of depreciation for human beings and their economies—for the credit we need to finance our lives, and collectively our communities. For us, however, in the industrial societies of the early twenty-first century, man is not the measure, and usury remains the rule by which we must live. For a viable alternative to the usurious financial system, we must look back 150 years, to the work of a little known American writer, Edward Kellogg, whose work is discussed in the next chapter.

Before we can consider what a non-usurious financial system like Kellogg's might look like, we need to complete our survey of the usurious economy. We need to understand in some detail how it has worked historically, especially more recently, to appreciate the damage it has caused, why it is so important to eliminate usury, and what the actual difference is between legitimate and usurious interest rates. We have been the victims historically of unnatural and arbitrary rates of interest, I have been arguing. Understanding these unnatural or usurious rates of interest is essential to understanding what a natural rate of interest might be, and why it is important. The history of modern credit has been one of persistently high interest rates, and other abuses of credit. The most secure debts, such as government bonds, have generally commanded over time 3 to 5 percent interest per year, and other kinds of debt often much more. Even when central bank lending rates (to major commercial banks) have been very low, sometimes close to zero, the relending rates of the commercial banks to businesses and the public—which is what really counts—have remained high. The necessity of credit, and its availability at usurious rates of interest, but hardly on any other condition, has dictated, I have argued, what has become a worldwide growth dynamic. We will start by examining this growth dynamic, and then consider some of the usurious mechanisms behind it. This will give us a context for approaching the notion of a natural rate of interest.

This growth dynamic has an oscillating nature, often called the business cycle. The role of usurious credit is fundamental to understanding the business cycle, though this is not often recognized. There were no business cycles in subsistence, pre-industrial economies based on reciprocity, at least none beyond the seasons significant enough to be noticeable to most people. Only with the monetization of the agricultural economy in the eighteenth century in Britain do the first business cycles appear, following at first, as we have seen, the seasonal pattern of loans made to farmers in the spring for planting, to be paid off after the fall harvest. Bankers, flush with deposits after the fall harvest, would lend to non-agricultural commercial or industrial borrowers, as we've seen, who in turn would pay back in time for bankers to refund the farmers the next spring. Farmers got new access to capital not only for seeds, but for other improvements. But insofar as they did so with borrowed money they were compelled to increase production to the degree to which they had to repay their loans with interest, hence the improvements, made especially by larger landowners in eighteenth century Britain looking to boost production. They had to improve production to service their loans, but they also gained new opportunities for increased revenues from increased production, that is, for income to exceed debt and interest payments, while producers who resisted "growth through debt" found themselves losing market share. Soon manufacturers found themselves prisoners of the same dynamic. The usurious burden on borrowed capital with its double or nothing logic had a magnifying or multiplying effect—manifest mathematically by compound interest formulas—which it is hard to overstate. The need to produce an additional surplus to cover usurious interest created a whole new psychology, one invoking greater opportunity and greater risk, to be sure, but also provoking anxiety and clouding judgment. On the downside, the failure to make debt payments is compounded as well, with the accumulated burden of unpaid debt plus interest plunging unsuccessful producers further in the hole than otherwise would have been the case, thus further delaying recovery from a crash.

These effects of usurious finance and oscillating credit—the well-known boom and bust cycle—were evident early on; a good early illustration can be found in credit flows between Britain and its American colonies in the eighteenth century, which turned out to be a central factor in the American revolution. Many of the British colonies in America, led by Massachusetts and Pennsylvania, had experimented with land banks and paper currencies— publically issued token money. Initially, colonial governments otherwise strapped for cash issued paper notes in payment for the goods and services they purchased, and agreed to accept those same notes for payment of taxes. Later on they found they could create money more effectively and broadly by offering direct loans to citizens, who put up land as collateral. The weakness of the earlier system was the temptation by governments to inflate the currency; later token currencies based on land proved more stable. All these notes were simple paper issues, that is, fiat money, not backed by specie. As long as interest rates were relatively low, and especially lower than on money borrowed from London, these colonial issues of low-cost credit contributed to local prosperity. But they tended to be usurious as well. Pennsylvania, for example—which had the most developed colonial currency—charged 5 percent on its land bank loans, still a high rate, though low compared to the 8 percent or more charged for money borrowed in London.

This budding colonial financial independence irked the money centers in London. Pressure for reasserting British financial control over the colonies came from the City of London, which persuaded the British government to reimpose the British monetary system in America. It was to the advantage of British investors to invest in America, if they could, where low wages (slaves, indentured servants, etc.) and abundant resources assured cheap production costs and good returns. Should the colonists control their own currencies, and thereby be able to borrow from themselves instead of the British, those profits to the British would be lost. Through a series of acts of Parliament, especially the Currency Acts of 1751 and 1764, Britain effectively shut down the colonial monetary credit systems by demanding payments to be made in British pounds, which could be borrowed only at higher rates from London, ensuring a flow of money back to Britain

The result of this forced tie-in to the London money markets was a severe credit crunch and economic depression in the 1760s in the colonies. The failure of the colonists, after considerable efforts, to persuade the mother country to throw off this imposed monetary control was an important factor which led directly to the Revolution, and one overlooked by most historians to this day. This largely ignored interpretation of the Revolution is masterfully presented by Terry Bouton in his *Taming Democracy*, a history of the American Revolution seen through the lens of events in Pennsylvania. Bouton describes how the imposition of the British financial system brought on the depression of the 1760s in the colonies:

This terrible crush arrived first in the countryside, where ordinary farmers were smashed beneath the collapsing chain of transatlantic credit. Farmers had borrowed from country storekeepers, who had borrowed from Philadelphia merchants, who had borrowed from London merchants and manufacturers. When money became scarce, the full weight of this claim pounded down on farmers. As an editorial in a Philadelphia newspaper explained, English creditors pressed Philadelphia merchants to settle up, which 'obliged [them] to do the same with our debtors in the country.' Worse yet, many farmers had gone into debt during the [French and Indian] war when money was abundant and prices were high; now, as money became scarce, prices dropped and farmers could not sell their crops and livestock for enough to cover the debt. Having bought high and sold low, farmers were crushed when the 'great scarcity of money' made it so that the 'poor debtor cannot procure cash to pay off his creditor.'[6]

Americans won their political independence, but not their independence from usury. The usurious London financial markets were quickly replaced by the usurious Philadelphia, New York, and Boston financial markets, and soon a recognizable pattern developed. In the early stages of the cycle, bad crops would leave farmers unable to repay; the flow of credit would be disrupted; there would be less money available to lend to others, spending would drop, and industry and commercial activity would suddenly contract instead of grow as demand plummeted and loans were called in. By the end of the eighteenth century, however, as the usurious credit economy came to be based more on the industrial and less on the agricultural economy, new complex, non-seasonal credit cycles began to appear, with longer periods of relative prosperity followed by protracted periods of relative stagnation or depression. Anecdotal evidence, public perceptions, and record-keeping going back to the late eighteenth century suggest certain overall prosperous or boom periods, particularly in English-speaking countries—the 1790s, the 1820s, the 1850s and 1860s, the 1900s, the 1920s, the 1950s and 1960s, the 1990s—and corresponding depressed eras, or busts—the 1810s, the 1830s and 1840s, the 1880s and 1890s, the 1930s, the 1970s and 1980s, and the 2000s. Except during the most severe contracting phases, some growth generally continued even during downturns, albeit at lower rates than during the booms. Marginal producers were wiped out, but those who survived stood to gain from increased market share in the next round of the cycle, as industries were steadily consolidated. Some kind of oscillation of credit and debt over time is probably to be expected, but the effect of adding usurious rates to debt is to magnify dramatically both the upsides and the downsides.

One of the best known characterizations of these longer cycles is the so-called Kondratieff wave theory, named after the early twentieth century Russian economist Nikolai Kondratieff.[7] Kondratieff claimed to have found a 50–60 year cycle, which roughly corresponds to the peaks and troughs noted above. His projections were based on the rise and fall of wholesale prices in Britain, France, and the United States from the late eighteenth century onwards. The many variables affecting booms and busts make his rather elastic cycles unreliable as precise predictors; yet, though booms and busts may be significantly extended or curtailed due to unforeseen factors, it is undeniable that a notable degree of oscillation in economic growth roughly as he described it has been characteristic of industrial societies fueled by credit at high interest rates. This has been, through most of the industrial era, an uneven but mainly upward oscillation, a matter by and large of two steps forward and one step back. The periods of credit contraction, painful as they have been, generally did not wipe out all the gains in wealth and technology achieved in previous expansions. Enough capital and natural resources remained to eventually restart the credit cycle as new borrowers and consumers gradually appeared, and drive it higher—until now.

In the initial or growth phase of the cycle, the money supply is increased as credit is made available to borrowers willing and able to take on debt. This new money to loan is created by the usurious lending of the financial system, supported by the collateral put up by borrowers and backed up by the minimal reserve or capital requirements placed on banks. But, on the principal discovered by the goldsmiths, far more money can be lent out than is likely to be redeemed at any time. Borrowers gain confidence from the opportunities posed by new and attractive infusions of borrowed capital—opportunities they calculate will outweigh the costs and risks of the capital they borrow. They aim to beat the locked-in usurious interest rate, but whether or not they succeed they are obligated to pay that interest as well as the principal. This increase in the volume of credit is thus inherently inflationary; prices rise and production expands while interest rates tend to rise to keep pace with the increasing demand for new money by optimistic borrowers. Eventually, however, in the normal cycle, production catches up with consumption, inventories build up, opportunities are gradually exhausted, borrowers become more cautious, and returns on borrowed money begin to decline. We enter a phase where the economy plateaus, and is able to manage no more than slow or uneven growth, punctuated by declines in various sectors. Credit put out on the expectation of continued high returns from expansion increasingly comes up short as bad debts begin to pile up.

Gradually a deflationary trend sets in. Borrowers begin to default; demand for goods and services stalls or drops; commodity prices start to fall; and creditors seek to compensate for shrinking numbers of borrowers by lowering rates to entice more borrowers. The debt burden nonetheless continues to grow as major investors repeatedly try to jump-start the economy with more borrowed capital, but with less and less success. Financial risk-taking and speculation increase. Eventually, too many investors find themselves overextended in debt; it becomes more difficult to borrow or lend money, even at low rates. A tipping point is reached. Deleveraging sets in, often suddenly in a dramatic crash. Confidence collapses. The credit markets shrink and may even "freeze up" as debtors are forced into bankruptcy. A period of austerity reconcentrates remaining assets in fundamentals, and gradually—at least in past rounds of this cycle—real savings once more begin to accumulate; eventually a new group of more or less debt-free borrowers emerges, whose good credit, combined with pent-up demand and new opportunities, enables the cycle to restart once more. This is provided, of course, that resources remain plentiful relative to population and consumption.

Up until the Great Depression began in 1929, the credit cycle was based almost wholly on private finance. The economies of the leading industrial nations of the day—Great Britain and the United States—were *laissez-faire* economies, that is, finance and productive ownership was almost entirely in private hands. This was particularly true in the United States, where even central banking was effectively challenged by Jeffersonians and Jacksonians. But the financial capital of the era remained London, where private enterprise continued to be backed by a large national debt and the Bank of England. Private interests were predominant in other industrializing countries as well, such as France and Germany (though somewhat tempered in Germany's case by Bismarck's pioneering welfare insurance programs which created a larger government sector than elsewhere). Traditional dynastic empires such as Russia encouraged private foreign investment. In the decade 1919–29, to illustrate the dominance of private investment, United States Federal budget expenditures added up to only 4 percent of gross national product,[8] a level typical of earlier American history, except for brief spurts of spending accompanying the Civil War and World War I. The later introduced of necessity large-scale government borrowing and spending, which abated considerably in the 1920s but reappeared to stay with the Depression of the 1930s and World War II. By the 1950s United States government share of gross national product reached 30 percent, and is currently approaching 50 percent of gross national product. Since the 1930s the earlier *laissez-faire* economy has morphed into a mixed or Keynesian economy in which government spending based mostly on government debt funded by taxpayers has been used to expand the pool of debt far beyond what seems possible in a *laissez-faire* economy.

William F. Hixon nicely sums up this dynamic:

> A *laissez-faire* type economy eventually comes to grief because of the over indebtedness in the private sector due to borrowing from banks and others. A Keynesian type mixed economy does not come to grief until there exists intolerable over indebtedness in both the private and federal sectors and that takes a little longer. But a Keynesian type mixed economy is doomed to an eventual

liquidity crisis similar to that which overtook its predecessor type economy in 1929. The Keynesian type of mixed economy has a longer tether than a *laissez-faire* economy—but only a little longer.[9]

Thus, although the mixed economy was already more overextended in 1987 than the *laissez-faire* economy was in 1929, according to Hixon, no depression followed the 1987 crash.[10] The tether held. By the late 1980s massive liquidity had been injected into the system by the government, including the savings-and-loan and Chrysler bailouts as well as increased military spending in the final Cold War showdown with the Soviet Union. Subsequent crises—the collapse of a huge hedge fund in 1998, Long Term Capital Management, the Asian financial crisis of the late 1990s, the collapse of Enron, and the bursting of the dot-com bubble—were all absorbed by the mixed Keynesian system by putting out more and more liquidity.

The system continued to lumber along. Commercial banks issued many sub-prime mortgages to marginal borrowers in the early 2000s, when the Federal Reserve held interest rates very low. Those banks at the same time invented a process called securitization, in which they bundled mortgages into a variety of exotic debt instruments (so-called collateralized debt obligations, or CDOs, among others), and sold those instruments to other banks, hedge funds, and large investors. By 2006, the subprime mortgage crisis seriously undermined the swollen debt pyramid, and in September 2008 one key liquidation (Lehman Brothers) threatened global collapse. One frantic federal bailout after another—Freddie Mac and Fannie Mae, Federal Reserve guarantees to investment banks, TARP money, the AIG bailout, the auto companies, hedge funds, etc.—amounting to many trillions of dollars was suddenly necessary to keep the economy afloat. The Federal Reserve and Treasury Department ended up buying virtually worthless "toxic assets" at inflated prices to keep the financial system functioning, at the taxpayer's long term expense.

As of this writing, the federal government under the Obama administration has more or less concluded a massive program of bailouts for financial institutions and other corporate entities deemed "too big to fail," with uncertain prospects. The Federal Reserve has flooded the banking system with low-cost loans under the label of "quantitative easing," which those banks are able to use not so much to lend out at low rates to the public but to lock in profits by buying high interest treasury debt. The debt burden, in short, is being put on future taxpayers in the faith—increasingly dubious—that economic "growth" can resume. The real bottom line is that the underlying resources necessary to restart another debt cycle—for the first time since the industrial revolution began—are by many measures now inadequate to the task. The cheap energy sources in particular which have powered the industrial revolution, especially fossil fuels, have become increasingly difficult to access and remain prone to accident and pollution—witness the BP offshore explosion and massive oil spill in the Gulf of Mexico in the summer of 2010. Alternative renewable energies and new technologies remain largely hypothetical and undeveloped, and so far do not appear to be feasible on the scales required. We have tapped out conventional resources to the point, now widely recognized, where scarcity dictates that what remains will be increasingly expensive to exploit, relative to the past. In sum, resource depletion, pollution and climate change ensure that continued industrial development will add increasingly to the costs borne by communities and ecosystems. Even if a new source of cheap, clean energy were found and another growth cycle were ignited, further expansion of population and consumption globally would only further stress the ecological limits of the planet with regard to living space, soils and farmland, water, fisheries, forests, etc. The party, it seems, is over.[11]

Let us examine more closely some of the financial instruments and techniques characteristic of the major abuses of credit in recent decades, including those which precipitated the current financial crisis. Until the gold standard was abandoned domestically in 1933 in the United States, and internationally in 1971, the explosion in usurious credit still had a connection, however tenuous, with commodity money. Since then that connection has been severed and there is no longer an external brake on the issuance of money. In our fiat money system, money is now freely created by central banks like the Federal Reserve at their discretion. In the United States, the Treasury Department sells bonds to commercial banks which in turn sell them to the Federal Reserve. The Fed buys these bonds simply, in its own words, by "issuing a check on itself" to the banks.[12] This puts into circulation new money created out of nothing, which forms the base of the lending pyramid of fractional reserve banking. By adjusting its bond purchases (buying and selling them) the Fed can control this base money supply and indirectly influence interest rates. Although prominent Fed officials, including the Chairman, are appointed by the President, their long terms and freedom of action, coupled with the fact that other key officials are appointed by the large commercial banks which actually own the Fed, ensure that for all practical purposes the banking system controls its policies. The lack of any adequate backing for the issuance of money, and the lack of any significant public accountability for the Fed's actions, means that we have a privatized and largely unregulated monetary system run for private profit at public expense.

It is on this foundation that the usurious credit system operates today. Credit and usury are not fixed and simple arrangements but complex and often rapidly evolving sets of techniques, though certain fundamental operations reach far back in history. Perhaps the most fundamental of these techniques is leveraging: using other people's money to make money. An explosion of leveraging has marked the most recent stage of the usurious economy, characterized by new and ingenious ways of expanding the supply of debt money. As the *Wikipedia* —our current repository of conventional wisdom— puts it: "Financial leverage takes the form of a loan or other borrowings (debt), the proceeds of which are reinvested with the intent to earn a greater rate of return than the cost of interest." Leverage typically takes money borrowed at usurious rates and reinvests it, ratcheting up the risk involved in hopes of ever higher gains.

Here's an example, adapted from a financial website, of how leveraging works:

> Suppose you have $10,000 and borrow $90,000 to purchase a $100,000 house. You have a leverage ratio of 10:1—for every $10 of the asset, you've put in $1 of equity (your own money). If house prices rise by 10 percent, and you sell, how much do you make? At first blush we'd say 10 percent, which is true— but you made 10 percent on the entire $100,000. The house is now worth $110,000, and after paying your $90,000 debt you're left with $20,000. That 10 percent growth, with 10x leverage, becomes 100 percent profit on your initial investment! . . . Now what about the reverse—when the house falls 10 percent to $90,000? Well, we can sell the house for $90,000, pay off our loan ($90,000) and are left with... zero! A 10 percent dip in prices becomes a 100 percent loss of equity. We're wiped out! We get 10x the loss when prices go south. And if the house price falls 20 percent (impossible! improbable! unlikely!), we suffer a 200 percent loss. We lose our initial $10,000 and owe $10,000 beyond that (since, if we sell the house for $80,000, we must still repay the $90,000 loan). Hopefully the magnifying effect of borrowed money is becoming clear. You lose your equity when the investment drops 1/leverage ratio—in this case, 1/10 or 10 percent. With a 25x leverage ratio, the investment only needs to drop 4 percent in order to be wiped out. One way to think about it: you're paying for losses out of your own pocket, not the borrowed money (you always have to pay it back). Your pocket is only $1 of the $10, so once you lose it ($1 out of $10, or 10 percent) you are wiped out. Any more, and you're in debt. [13]

There are many ways to leverage debt in this way, but two in particular stand out historically: fractional reserve banking and derivatives. In fractional reserve banking, traced back in its modern form to the British goldsmiths of the seventeenth century, banks must retain in cash some fraction of their deposits (traditionally 10 percent, recently much less); the rest they are free to loan out. We can consider the deposits to be "loans" by customers to the bank, on which the bank pays some interest, though less than what it can make by relending the money. When the loaned out money is redeposited, not necessarily in the bank of origin but somewhere in the banking system, given a 10 percent reserve ratio, then 90 percent of it can be loaned out again, and so on, until the diminishing multiplier effect of the original deposit is exhausted.

This dynamic is worth spelling out: A $100,000 deposit in a bank allows it to lend out $90,000; the redeposit of that $90,000 in it or another bank allows another $81,000 to be lent out, and so on, adding up to a total of almost $9 million in possible dollars lent out in the banking system as whole on an initial deposit of $100,000, for an overall leverage ratio in the system of 90-1. Bankers long ago discovered that they can use someone else's (their depositors') money as a collateral base to support a hugely expanded money supply. They make their money off the interest they charge on the new money they create by the loans they make. And they compound the process with each new level of lending, charging interest over and over on what is essentially the same money.

Fractional reserve banking is a classic example of multiplying money through leveraging, though not usually described as such, and it has been central to modern economies. In sum, bankers "borrow" depositors money and reloan it, albeit without their explicit knowledge or approval, not once, but many times over. Under normal circumstances, fractional reserve banking is not as dangerous as it sounds at first blush, since the money loaned out over and over is redeposited back into the banking system. But the system as a whole remains vulnerable: if enough depositors across the board lose confidence and demand their money, the whole thing will collapse. An investor or business person or entrepreneur also uses leverage, that is, invests other peoples' money is hopes of profiting in the end. But the banker, unlike the normal investor, produces nothing in the process but nonetheless collects a fee (interest) by exercising a monopolistic right to create money through loans. Bankers argue that the loan capital they provide is a necessary service, but, as we shall see, loan capital can in fact otherwise be provided without a gratuitous payment to the providers.

Fractional reserve banking has been the dominant instrument for expanding credit since the financial revolution, and it continues to underpin the system today. It is derivatives, however, which in recent decades have taken the lead in credit expansion. Widespread use of derivatives dates from the closing decades of the twentieth century, with the rise of hedge funds. The era of deregulation, beginning under President Jimmy Carter in the United States in the 1970s and continued by his successors—an era when much of the transparency and accountability as existed previously was removed—opened the door to these new financial instruments. A derivative is a specialized kind of debt, a contractual obligation to buy or sell some asset at some future date and price, or an option to do so; it is a future value *derived* (hence the name) from an asset as a projection (up or down) of its current value. Derivatives facilitate hedging, that is, finding counterparties to share risk, and so can be understood as a kind of insurance. Various kinds of "creative" derivative financing, such as credit default swaps (CDs), first widely revealed to the public in the aftermath of the collapse of the Enron Corporation in 2000, helped allow debt obligations (futures contracts) against current assets to be kept off the books. The unregulated, totally privatized, and 'over the counter' opaque derivatives market not only permitted futures contracts to be repackaged and bid up far beyond their current market value, but also permitted them to function as a hidden, unregulated, shadow banking system, mostly free of public accountability. Derivatives were commonly private contracts, privately exchanged, with no public registration or marketplace. As a result, the financial system and the economy it supported became ever harder to understand and predict, dramatically increasing uncertainty and risk.

The *Wikipedia* gives a typical example of how derivatives are supposed to work:

> a wheat farmer and a miller . . . sign a futures contract to exchange a specified amount of cash for a specified amount of wheat in the future. . . . the farmer and the miller both reduce a risk and acquire a risk when they sign the futures contract: The farmer reduces the risk that the price of wheat will fall below the price specified in the contract and acquires the risk that the price of wheat will rise above the price specified in the contract (thereby losing additional income that he could have earned). The miller, on the other hand, acquires the risk that the price of wheat will fall below the price specified in the contract (thereby paying more in the future than he otherwise would) and reduces the risk that the price of wheat will rise above the price specified in the contract. In this sense, one party is the insurer (risk taker) for one type of risk, and the counter-party is the insurer (risk taker) for another type of risk.

So far there is no cause for complaint. As long as the actual trading of the assets or commodities in question in the real market approximates the dollar value of the derivatives of those assets or commodities, then the derivative price remains anchored in the real world, and can't drift too far from evidence-based market prices. But once derivatives exceed in dollar value the current market value of the original items in question, as they long since have, then the derivative tail begins to wag the dog of the real economy. How could that happen? Once a market for derivatives was created, primarily by the major banks, then they could be bought and sold. This was done by separating ownership of derivatives from ownership of the underlying assets. It's one thing for the farmer and the miller to exchange futures contracts, or derivatives, for their mutual protection. It's quite another thing for such contracts to be detached from them and sold to third parties in an anonymous market. Once that happens, speculators are free to bid up prices of derivatives in repeated resales far beyond the real value of the underlying asset. Moreover, this can be done by buying derivatives with borrowed money. Derivatives now can be leveraged many times over, creating vast financial pyramids.[14] According to the International Swaps and Derivative Association (ISDA), the notional value of global derivatives in 2006 totaled \$283 trillion, as against a world economic output of about \$40 trillion. Other estimates run even higher, to well over \$1 quadrillion.

This surge was facilitated in part by an April 2004 ruling by the Securities and Exchange Commission which allowed big investment banks to increase their debt-to-capital ratio from 12:1 to 30:1, and even higher under certain circumstances. Insofar as a derivative is a kind of a debt, one which typically delays a transaction over weeks or months but nonetheless obligates it, the explosion in derivatives not only added to overall debt burden, already exaggerated by forms of usurious lending, but compounded it even further. Derivatives, as the well-known investor Warren Buffet famously put it, are "financial weapons of mass destruction." They have come to constitute a vast sea of exponentially leveraged debt obligations far in excess of the productive value of the real economy. A sudden downturn, such as that sparked by defaults in the sub-prime mortgage market, can unravel the whole system just as exponentially. A crucial element in the crash of 2008 was the failure of the American Insurance Group (AIG), the largest insurance company, to meet \$18 billion in derivative obligations, which would have set off a much larger, massive chain reaction. We can now appreciate, after the crash of 2008, how a derivatives debt market many times the size of the world economy could have been created outside the public view. We see here a scheme in which more and more investors put their money, or allowed Wall Street speculators to put their money, betting that even more new investors would follow them and further bid up the price. Leveraging is a modified ponzi-scheme, modified for the worse in that a small amount of equity underwrites leveraging a mountain of debt, as opposed to none at all, as for instance in a chain letter. The key presumption is one of further, indeed endless growth, without which the system would collapse.

The financial economy did well in the boom years of the computer-and-internet explosion—from the mid-1980s to the early 2000s—when innovation and actual economic growth made expectations of huge returns on minimal investment plausible. But the computer-and-internet revolution eventually slowed down, while resource depletion, particularly in energy led by oil, made further growth problematic. The sub-prime mortgage crisis in 2007 was an early signal that expectations of continued growth might not be sustained; but perhaps as important was the astronomical run-up in oil and commodity prices. Crude oil prices rose from \$64/barrel in August of 2007 to \$147/barrel in July 2008, signaling to buyers that ponzi schemes based on derivatives trading in oil were likely to contract rather than continuing to expand. The oil price spike suggested that the limits of oil production had been reached, or at least anticipated, and that demands of a growth economy for energy would less likely be met in the future. Investors began to pull back across the board. If it is true that no combination of alternative energies so far can hope to make up more than a fraction of the energy provided by oil, and if this became evident to key investors, particularly the large banks, they will begin to sell (if they can) their outstanding assets to cover their financial speculations in order to remain solvent—a self-feeding, ongoing, relentless process which leads to bankruptcies, unemployment, etc. There appears to be no real remedy in sight, though government bailouts have propped up the banking system as of this writing. If we take the $283 trillion indicated above as the 2006 value of all derivatives (compared to the over $1 quadrillion some analysts claim), and $40 trillion as the value of the 2006 world economy, and if we assume debt ought not to exceed collateral, we are left with an excess of $243 trillion to wring out of the system, which may be a conservative estimate. That number ought to boggle the mind.

The crash of 2008 was largely due to the unwinding of leveraged derivatives, and their collapse at first promised to be as exaggerated as their rise. Disaster was averted only by a bailout of the largest banks and major corporations by the government and the Federal Reserve to the tune of over $10 trillion. This was disclosed only two years later, and only as part of a financial regulation passed by Congress in 2010. The result has been to transfer the massive debt burden to taxpayers, where it remains today. The credit markets, however, continue to be slow if not frozen as lenders see few profitable risks in an economy stalled out on economic growth. The phase of government bailouts temporarily stabilized the falling economy, postponing but not evading the day of reckoning. In fact they arguably only made it worse. In the Depression, the option of tapping the taxpayer was still available; at that time personal and government debt was relatively small. That option today is largely played out, with personal, corporate, and government debt at all time highs. Unlike the 1930s, resource depletion, climate change, and overpopulation today leave little room for renewed growth. The not so subtle message of "peak oil" is that there are no more "cheap" resources to exploit to sustain economic growth. The further extraction of fossil fuels, including deep water, shale oil, shale gas, tar sands, mountaintop coal, etc., can be achieved only by ever more expensive technologies and ever more expensive damage to the environment and other economic assets and activities. This realization, perhaps more than any other, encapsulated by the $147 peak oil price of 2008, made plain to many investors that the expected high rates of return on their investment would not be forthcoming, hence the selloff and collapse of the debt markets, and their inability to absorb what might otherwise have been manageable losses in subprime mortgages—the trigger of the crisis. The industrial growth economy, fueled by usurious interest rates, seems finally to have reached its Malthusian limits.

Finally, the political implications of usurious debt should be noted. The exploited debtor, as opposed to that earlier model of exploitation—the industrial laborer—has internalized his or her obligation. The rhetoric of individualistic freedom dovetails nicely with the personal moral imperative to repay one's debts, making any mass resistance to the usurious economy that much more difficult. The debtor is bound into a system into which he or she appears to enter into a free contract, but as a practical matter often has little choice. Any pushback from the public is thereby muted, leaving creditors a free hand to pursue their interests. This disjunction suggests why there is so little political opposition to the usurious economic system. It also suggests its profound weakness: the lack of constructive feedback leaves those in control without any corrective mechanism to check their excesses. A recent author, Maurizio Lazzarato, puts it this way: "What puts us at risk . . . is not the complexity of the technical-socio-economic infrastructure, but the fact that the process for evaluating and deciding is detached from any kind of democratic challenge or validation and exercised instead by minority (financial, economic, political, etc.) groups, which, given their very position, are utterly 'unqualified.'"[15] The risks of the new complexity, we might demur, are real enough, as we have been arguing, but the lack of political channels open to dealing with them insures that they are not likely to be dealt with rationally.

NOTES

1. William F. Hixon, *A Matter of Interest: Reexamining Money, Debt, and Real Economic Growth* (New York: Praeger, 1991).

2. Ibid., p. 15.

3. Ibid., p. 19.

4. Ibid., pp. 23–4

5. Ibid., p. 62.

6. Terry Bouton, *Taming Democracy: The People, the Founders, and the Troubled Ending of the American Revolution* (Oxford: Oxford University Press, 2007), p. 22.

7. Nikolai Kondratieff, "The Long Waves in Economic Life," trans. W. F. Stolper, in *The Review of Economic Statistics*, vol. XVII, no. 6, Nov. 1935, pp. 105–15.

8. Ibid, p. 142.

9. Ibid., p. 127.

10. Hixon writes: "The *laissez-faire* system broke down in 1929 when the PII/TPI [personal interest income/total personal income] amounted to only a little over 8 percent. In the mixed economy of 1985, the ratio soared to nearly 15 percent without generating a protest movement of any consequence on the part of either entrepreneurs or wage earners. Only time will tell what the limit is to their spirit of toleration." *A Matter of Interest* (see note 1 above), p. 239. As of this writing, over 20 years later, we are still waiting.

11. A recent general summary of global resource depletion and its undercutting of economic growth can be found in Richard Heinberg's *The End of Growth* (Gabriola Island: New Society Publishers, 2011), *et passim.*

12. *The Federal Reserve System: Purposes & Functions,* Board of Governors of the Federal Reserve System (Washington, DC, 1994), pp. 35–6; see also Chris Martenson, *The Crash Course* (Hoboken: John Wiley & Sons, 2011), pp. 47–49.

13. http://betterexplained.com/articles/understanding-debt-risk-and-leverage/ posted Nov. 17, 2008.

14. Michael Lewis gives as good a summary of how this was done as this writer has seen: "In a mortgage bond, you gathered thousands of loans and, assuming that it was extremely unlikely that they would all go bad together, created a tower of bonds, in which both risk and return diminished as you rose. In a CDO [collateralized debt obligation] you gathered one

hundred different mortgage bonds—usually, the riskiest, lower floors of the original tower—and used them to erect an entirely new tower of bonds. The innocent observer might reasonably ask, What's the point of using floors from one tower of debt simply to create another tower of debt? The short answer is, they are too near to the ground. More prone to flooding—the first to take losses—they bear a lower credit rating: triple-B. Triple-B-rated bonds were harder to sell than the triple-A-rated ones, on the safe, upper floors of the building.

"The long answer was that there were huge sums of money to be made, if you could somehow get them re-rated as triple-A, thereby lowering their perceived risk, however dishonestly and artificially. This is what Goldman Sachs had cleverly done. Their—soon to be everyone's—nifty solution to the problem of selling the lower floors appears, in retrospect, almost magical. Having gathered 100 ground floors from 100 different subprime mortgage buildings (100 different triple-B-rated bonds), they persuaded the rating agencies that these weren't, as they might appear, all exactly the same things. They were another diversified portfolio of assets! This was absurd. The 100 buildings occupied the same floodplain; in the event of flood, the ground floors of all of them were equally exposed. But never mind: The rating agencies, who were paid fat fees by Goldman Sachs and other Wall Street firms for each deal they rated, pronounced 80 percent of the new tower of debt triple-A.

"The CDO was, in effect, a credit laundering service for the residents of Lower Middle Class America. For Wall Street it was a machine that turned lead into gold. "Michael Lewis, *The Big Short: Inside the Doomsday Machine* (New York: W. W. Norton, 2010), p. 73.

15. Maurizio Lazzarato, *The Making of the Indebted Man* (Amsterdam: Semiotext, 2011), p. 143.

Chapter Seven

The People's Money

Having inveighed against the pernicious nature of the privatized usurious financial system—"the English system"—I owe the reader some kind of solution to the problems I have raised. Is another, better financial system possible? The system under which we suffer is so pervasive, so large in scale, and so deeply rooted, that any alternative seems inconceivable, even to most educated people. We should remember, however, that this system, although dating back to the early eighteenth century in Britain, established itself relatively recently and only after a long struggle in the United States, where down to the end of the nineteenth century it was strongly resisted by powerful political forces. The nature of the monetary system—whether it should be public or private, usurious or non-usurious, centralized or decentralized—was a live political issue in America from colonial times to the 1890s, and to lesser extent down through the Depression era. Public controversies centered over land banks, colonial currencies, Hamilton's national debt and central banking ideas, Jackson's famous veto of the Bank of the United States, free banking, the introduction of Greenbacks, the gold standard, the difficulty of obtaining credit by farmers, artisans, and ordinary citizens after the Civil War, social credit schemes, etc. In this era colonial radicals, antifederalists, Jeffersonians, Jacksonians, Greenbackers, mutualists, and nineteenth-century populists all resisted the encroaching power of the privatized, centralized, usurious money system. These critics were defeated by the plutocratic forces they called "the money power," who managed to devise and implement a system designed to employ other peoples' wealth to make vast private fortunes; in the end, "the money power" managed to gain effective control over the political system, mainly by funding lobbyists, bribing politicians, and directing propaganda campaigns defending the interests of wealthy elites, the "free enterprise" system, bankers and investors, corporate power, and the

97

methods of Wall Street.[1] The populist Peoples Party of the 1890s—which elected 50 representatives to Congress, along with numerous state and local officials—was the last serious political resistance to usury and "the money power" in the United States, and its defeat in that decade signaled the decisive victory of the plutocrats, whose reign continues to this day.

This is not the place to rehearse that history in detail. But we find among these critics of the privatized usurious monetary system serious and well thought out alternatives. The most fully developed and compelling of these alternative monetary theories, in my view, is found in the work of Edward Kellogg (1790–1858), an American who developed an extraordinary monetary theory, one designed to evade the evils of usury while allowing for a democratically controlled, decentralized but broadly coordinated monetary system able to provide credit to individuals without forcing them to produce at unsustainable levels to meet their obligations. Kellogg's ideas—unique in developing the notion of a sustainable, decentralized yet nationally standardized, and non-usurious monetary system—are worth considering in detail. I offer them here as a practical template for a financial system consistent with social justice and a sustainable economy. By a practical template I mean not an exhaustive blueprint but a first and general approximation of a possible monetary system designed to serve these ends. Given the importance of his ideas and their unfamiliarity to most readers, I shall quote Kellogg at length in what follows.

Edward Kellogg was a New York City businessman whose losses in the crash of 1837 led him to reexamine the business cycle, monetary policy, and debt. In a series of works, Kellogg developed the idea of distributing capital to the public not by 'taking' from the rich through taxes and other direct appropriations—as widely advocated by socialists, progressives, liberals and other leftists—but by abolishing usurious interest rates and having the government set a standard of very low or nominal interest loans to individual citizens. He determined that these loans, to be the basis of a new monetary system he called The Safety Fund, would have to have a uniform, fixed interest rate established by law nationally. They would be issued locally, however, not nationally, through a system of community-based public credit banks. There would be no central bank in the modern sense, only a central regulatory agency ensuring that local issuance of loans would be consistent and according to uniform standards from place to place. Once issued, these low-interest loan notes would circulate as currency, replacing the privately-issued, high-interest banking notes of his day (which today take the form of Federal Reserve Notes). Although Kellogg wrote newspaper articles and essays in Horace Greeley's *Tribune* and elsewhere, and published a book in 1849 entitled *Labor and Other Capital*, his views are most fully developed in his posthumous work, *A New Monetary System*, edited by his daughter, Mary Kellogg Putnam, and published in 1861. In his day he seems to have influenced even Abraham Lincoln who, according to historian Mark A. Lause, " . . . had his own copy of Kellogg's book, *Labor and Capital [sic]* advocating the government issuance of paper currency as a just means of redistributing wealth, and he corresponded with the author's son-in-law."[2] In spite of this, Kellogg's ideas were only partly understood in his time, and are mostly forgotten today.

Kellogg's public currency was intended to end the monopoly over the discretionary issuance of money at interest held then (and now) by the private banking and investment system. Since capital is available to most of us only by borrowing at varying rates of interest from private creditors, mostly banks, and since creditors are free by and large to charge whatever rates the market will bear, they are in a strong position to command interest as a premium for their loans. Through payment of this interest, populists and others argued, wealth is steadily concentrated in the hands of creditors. With a system of public credit such as Kellogg's, however, no such private premium need be necessary; benefits of a loan, if any, would accrue to the debtor, not the creditor. Kellogg aimed to replace what he called private "usurious" money with public, non-usurious money, allowing the general public access to capital without paying any kind of tribute for it. This dispersion of capital on accessible and favorable terms would itself strongly mitigate against its concentration in few hands. Kellogg's vision of non-usurious low interest public capital for all inspired nineteenth-century greenbackers, populists, and others who sought to restructure the monetary system to redistribute wealth; but none of them presented as thoroughgoing an analysis of public credit as Kellogg himself.[3] Unlike Kellogg, most of them favored a centralized monetary system under direct government control, a view still popular in progressive political circles today. In our own time, a time when credit in the form of private finance capital remains the dominant force in economic life, and is largely taken for granted even by educated people, the decentralized populist alternative Kellogg offers is arguably more important than ever. Kellogg's new monetary system was designed as a remedy for the economic injustice of the mal-distribution of wealth; what is remarkable— especially for our purposes, as we shall see—is that it also promises to be an antidote to the reckless and destructive economic "growth" which has brought us to an eco-crisis which only a few rare minds in Kellogg's day, such as Malthus and Darwin, might have anticipated.

Let us begin with Kellogg's own summary of his system: "In the plan we are about to propose for the formation of a National Currency by the General Government," he tells us,

> all the money circulated in the United States will be issued by a national institution [The Safety Fund], and will be a representative of actual property, therefore it can never fail to be a good and safe tender in payment of debts. It

will be loaned to individuals in every State, county, and town, at a uniform rate of interest, and hence will be of invariable value throughout the Union. All persons who offer good and permanent security will be at all times supplied with money, and for any term of years during which they will regularly pay the interest. Therefore, no town, county, or State, need be dependent upon any other for money, because each has real property enough to secure many times the amount which it will require. If more than the necessary amount of money be issued, the surplus will be immediately funded, and go out of use without injury. It will be impossible for foreign nations, or any number of banks, or capitalists, to derange the monetary system, either by changing the rate of interest, or by inducing a scarcity or a surplus of money. It will be the duty of the Government to ascertain as nearly as possible what rate of interest will secure to labor and capital their respective rights, and to fix the interest at that rate.[4]

"The money [itself] will bear no interest," he goes on to add,

but may always be exchanged for the Safety Fund Notes, which will bear interest. Those who may not wish to purchase property or pay debts with their money, can always loan it to the Institution for a Safety Fund Note, bearing an interest of one percent. per annum. Therefore the money will always be good for it will be the legal tender for debts and property, and can always be invested to produce an income. The money being loaned at one and one-tenth percent, and the Safety Fund Notes bearing but one percent, the difference . . . will induce owners of money to lend to individuals, and thus prevent continual issuing and funding of money by the Institution.[5]

Kellogg's summary needs explication. Just how would his system work? He proposed that local public credit banks be established, and we might imagine one in each county, and perhaps in each community or neighborhood. These local public credit banks would be part of a national system he called The Safety Fund. Instead of money being issued (as it is now) through a centralized money management system on a discretionary, top-down basis, primarily as loans from a central bank to major commercial banks, and then to regional and local banks, and finally to the public on the basis of fractional reserve lending and capital reserves, money in his system would be supplied on demand by what he called The Principal Institution of The Safety Fund to the independent, decentralized, local member banks of the Fund. This issuance by the Principal Institution would not be discretionary, but rather made on demand by the local branches according to their needs. The local public credit banks would be the ones who would actually issue money as loans directly to the public, that is, to citizens at a nominal but standardized interest rate on the basis of the economic prospects of those citizens. These member or branch banks, federally authorized and monitored but locally run, would offer low interest loans to individual citizens at a fixed rate, backed by good collateral. *These loan notes would be the only source of money in circulation.*

Kellogg lived in a largely pre-corporate world, compared to today, and he presumed that only flesh-and-blood persons could borrow money from public credit banks. And although he allowed only land as collateral for his loans, today we might consider other reliable assets, perhaps including a person's anticipated lifetime earning capacity. At the low interest rate on which he insisted—a key point of his system, of which more below—such loans would be more likely to be repaid and thereby more secure than those with higher rates. Once lent out, Kellogg's public credit dollars would flow into circulation, constituting a new currency backed by the assets of individual borrowers. The beauty of Kellogg's system lies in its decentralized but standardized, self-regulating nature. The federal government's role would *not* be to run a central bank as we know it, or vary interest rates or issue (or withdraw) money as it pleased—here Kellogg parts company with today's received wisdom, including that of liberal and progressive reformers. The government's role would be simply to fix the standard and assure the supply of locally-issued money. *Indeed, there would be no central bank at all in the current understanding of the term, and no need of one.* The Principal Institution would serve the local banks, not dictate to them, in matters of money creation; at the same time, it would make sure they operated according to a common set of rules.

Let us explain further. The Safety Fund consists of a national regulatory agency, what Kellogg called the Principal Institution, and its local branches, or member banks. The Principal Institution would regulate the local member banks by making sure they applied uniform standards of issuance of loans and abided by other common standards. It would provide local banks with currency at their request, but the actual issuance of currency would be at the discretion of local banks in response to local demand for loans. The ability of The Principal Institution to refuse to provide currency to local banks for loans is a disciplinary mechanism necessary to prevent those banks from abusing their powers. This function should not be confused with traditional central bank operation. The Safety Fund would *not* issue money at its discretion, which is the principal function of a central bank. Instead it would be obliged to give local banks the funds they requested as long as those local banks operated by the rules. The actual issuance of money would be decided entirely at the local level, with The Principal Institution acting as an umpire over a self-managing decentralized financial system, not as its director. Unlike a central bank, the Principal Institution, coordinating the system nationally, would not lend at interest at all, nor would it lend preferentially to some borrowers rather than others; nor would it have any discretionary power to direct the system, apart from enforcing uniform legal standards, above all, the fixed interest rate. There would be no need for fractional reserve lending. The Principal Institution, in short, would have *no control over the money supply*. No one would. Instead the money supply would be determined automatically through countless independent decisions by various citizens borrowing money for many different reasons in numerous and widely dispersed local public credit banks.

On the national level, instead of a central institution creating money, we would have one defining money, while leaving it to its branches to create it. Kellogg located this function revealingly not in any central bank at all, but in the national Bureau of Standards, whose job would be not to create money but to enforce its value through maintaining by law a perpetually fixed 1.1 percent interest rate. In his words: "The Safety Fund may consist of a Principal Institution with Branches," and that "the Principal Institution should issue money only to the Branches."[6] The issuance of currency *only* to the branches, and presumably *only* upon their demand, is what would enable the Principal Institution to monitor local practices and enforce the law; but this also prohibits it from issuing money to anyone else. A branch found in violation of national monetary standards (perhaps by charging illegal interest rates, refusing loans on good collateral, embezzling depositors' money, or otherwise defrauding the public) could be deprived of new currency to issue until reorganized on a sound basis. A local federal credit bank issuing too many bad loans, or refusing loans to otherwise credit-worthy citizens, would presumably be subject to legal action and legal penalties, including closure and reorganization. Without such a provision, we would have an unregulated system of anarchic free banking. National standards, in addition, would determine for The Safety Fund uniform rules of credit-worthiness, rules of local public management, and other technical matters.

The Safety Fund with its Principal Institution and its local branches would not constitute a banking system as we understand it today. In Kellogg's words:

> It is not intended that the Safety Fund and its Branches shall be made offices of discount and deposit. If they should be made such, they would more than double the amount of their loans; but the increase of loans would not augment the amount of money. They would lend the money left on deposit, and thus increase their income, as banks now lend their deposits and gain the interest.[7]

When he says that public credit banks should not be made offices of discount and deposit, he means they ought not to be in the traditional banking business of making loans on deposit at all, much less on the basis of fractional reserve banking. Kellogg fears much harm not only in the prospect of fractional reserve banking, but in any loans on deposits at all. For this reason he rules out making deposits at public credit banks, and recommends that those who wish to park their money do so by buying Safety Fund bonds at 1 percent.[8] (He does not address the convenience—no doubt not so much felt in his day—of having simple, demand deposit accounts in place of having to buy bonds; perhaps Safety Fund branches could accept such deposits, provided no loans were made on them, and interest were paid at one percent. These are important but technical details to be resolved in any serious application of Kellogg's system.)

How is the Principal Institution to define money? How is it to regulate the system without dominating it? Kellogg maintains that we can define a dollar in terms of the interest rate it can command: "The worth and amount of the interest on the dollar," Kellogg tells us,

> constitute and determine the value of the dollar. . . . Demand and supply are sometimes said to give value to money; but it would be as reasonable to assert that demand and supply fix the length of the yard, the weight of the pound. . . . Money is valuable in proportion to its power to accumulate value by interest. A dollar which can be loaned for twelve percent interest is worth twice as much as one that can be loaned for but six percent; just as a railroad stock which will annually bring in twelve percent is worth twice as much as one that annually brings in six percent. [9]

A dollar of fixed value would be one with a fixed interest rate. A dollar of sustainable value would be one with a sustainable fixed interest rate. To achieve the purpose of a stable currency, Kellogg insisted that this rate be fixed by law in perpetuity, and enforced by The Principal Institution—perhaps today it would take a constitutional amendment.

Kellogg determined that this fixed, permanent interest rate ought to be 1.1 percent. Why 1.1 percent? A one percent rate of interest, we might recall, was the limit on interest established by the Council of Nicaea in the fourth century; any rate beyond that was condemned as usurious. But, most fundamentally, one percent, as we have seen in the last chapter, is equivalent to the natural depreciation rate of a human life, that is, the replacement production necessary to maintain a steady state economy for us over the course of time. Kellogg is very precise on this number: "A rate of interest of even two percent per annum," he tells us, would put it out of the power of the people to fulfill their contracts. The establishment of this rate of interest would be equivalent to the passing of a law, compelling the laboring classes to double the capital of a nation, in favor of capitalists once in thirty-four and a half years, besides producing their own support. . . . Would not a tribute or tax like this keep us forever in poverty?"[10] The 1.1 percent rate, he argues in effect, is justified not only because it is fairly redistributive of capital, but because it is the rate which allows for the replacement of resources over a lifetime; it sustains a natural rate of consumption which avoids over-consuming as well as under-consuming our resources. We have already suggested, in light of the rule of 72, that approximately one percent is a natural or sustainable replacement rate for resources insofar as it is the replacement measure for a lifetime; if that is so, we can arrive at a replacement measure for society by applying the 1.1 percent rate to all borrowing. With individuals all borrowing at a replacement rate, society will in effect do so as well.

If I borrow $100,000 at 1.1 percent, then to discharge my obligation I will end up paying back a total of $200,000 over sixty years (approximating a working lifetime), leaving the public credit bank with twice the amount of money it originally lent out. Once created, a note from The Safety Fund (like any coin or note) would be virtually perpetual (though it might be lost or destroyed); it would continue to be used repeatedly as a claim on resources in the marketplace. To avoid endlessly inflating the currency, therefore, money must be extinguished as well as created; to that end, the public credit bank must write down paid-off debts. In our case, the $100,000 in principal would be extinguished as it is repaid—that is, it would not be counted as an asset for the bank, or relent in any way, but cancelled out as simply as it was created. The $100,000 of interest, however, would be left to the bank to lend out again to replace, in effect, the goods and services consumed over sixty years. In this way, the public credit system would be continuously recapitalized as it was being consumed. The 1.1 percent interest rate would establish a perpetual economic steady-state consonant with living on renewable resources.

Notice that if I borrow at zero rather than 1.1 percent, I do not provide for the replacement of my house or other resources, only for their consumption. Consider a house as a symbol for all the resources society as a whole consumes, including one's share in them. If the principal only were repaid (zero percent interest), money would be extinguished but not renewed, inducing a perpetual deflationary spiral. Local public credit banks under these circumstances, once all available collateral was pledged as debt, would not be able to lend; no future projects could be funded, no matter how desperately needed. The economy would steadily contract. The 1.1 percent interest, by contrast with no interest, requires that debtors work not only to support their own consumption, but that they also contribute at a moderate pace, over a lifetime, to replenish "'the capital of the nation," that is, the capital of nature, as we might put it today, which they have used up, in order to continue consumption by their descendents. This is arguably a fair return to society, which, after all, through its earlier labors, made the original loan possible.

To borrow money, it cannot be overemphasized, is to borrow a claim against the goods and services available in the marketplace. Speculation apart, money borrowed is cashed-in and put to work for some practical purpose; otherwise there would be little point to borrowing in the first place. Putting borrowed money to work means that resources will be consumed, and therefore diminished, for whatever purposes the borrower has in mind. Those resources must somehow be replenished by the borrower to the value of the original loan. Beyond this, in Kellogg's system, the borrower is free to retain any surplus he or she might manage to produce through utilizing the resources commanded by the borrowed money. The borrower in the usurious economy, by contrast, ends up having to consume resources far beyond his or her own needs, without any provision to replace them, thus breaking what should be a closed or balanced cycle of consumption and replenishment.

Kellogg's ingenious solution to cover this fatal loophole—his proposed 1.1 percent interest rate—ensures that *all not just some of the resources consumed as a result of borrowing are replenished.* It does so by insisting that the pool of credit is maintained to compensate for the natural rate of resource depletion, given the average span of a human lifetime. Our current system charges too much interest, and worse, diverts it into private hands, so that excess "growth" is commanded by a few who accrue the benefits, not the many who must labor to make it happen. In the process, resources are depleted, not maintained, and nature left diminished. Kellogg's system charges just the right amount of interest, a natural rate of interest, if you will, just what is needed to balance consumption—not too much and not too little—and it ensures that credit is not privatized but made available to all in a public system in which society as a whole, in countless, independent transactions, lends money to itself instead of a few lending to the many. Insofar as society is enriched by productive activity, the new wealth thus created in turn becomes collateral for further borrowing, the money supply thus naturally keeping pace with any increase in wealth—and vice-versa in the case of a decrease in wealth. The limits to wealth creation are the natural limits of what can be done with finite resources. The Kelloggian, steady-state economy will grow if resources and population permit, or contract if there is overshoot, but the one thing it will not do is demand "growth" beyond what resources allow.

A sustainable or steady-state economy, in sum, is no more or less than a replacement economy (given current resource limits) over the course of a lifetime, which, following Kellogg, can be defined—insofar as far as the monetary system is concerned—at about one percent interest on money, the rate which allows a population to reproduce over the lifetimes of its members the goods and services it consumes, leaving to posterity not a perpetually increasing debt, nor a contracting economy, but a material legacy equivalent to that with which it began. Holding to this standard for succeeding generations would establish a sustainable financial system designed to run indefinitely. Such, at least, is the promise of Kellogg's system, a promise important enough to be taken seriously. An unsustainable or "growth" economy by contrast requires the debtor to repay the lender at rates not only exceeding the replacement value of current production, but often exceeding even the rate at which an economy is able to grow even by maximizing its labor and resources. Kellogg puts it nicely: ". . . the present rates of interest greatly exceed the increase of wealth by natural production, and consequently, call for production beyond the ability of producers to supply."[11]

This debt burden on the economy would be eliminated with Kellogg's public credit funding at 1.1 percent interest. His loans would put capital into people's pockets and decentralize and personalize productivity. In his day, there was still an abundance of resources and plenty of room to grow. As he put it:

> In the United States, if interest were reduced to one, or to one and one-tenth percent, useful productions would probably increase from twenty-five to fifty percent. The wealth, instead of being accumulated in a few hands, would be distributed among producers. A large proportion of the labor employed in building up cities would be expended in cultivating and beautifying the country. Internal improvements would be made to an extent, and in a perfection unexampled in the history of nations. Agriculture, manufactures, and the arts would flourish in every part of the country. Those who are now non-producers would naturally become producers. The production would be owned by those who performed the labor, because the standard of distribution would nearly conform to the natural rights of man. [12]

And further, he adds:

> The percentage income upon capital can only be paid with the proceeds of labor; therefore this reduction of the percentage income would be equivalent to the distribution of several hundred millions of dollars among the producing classes, according to the labor performed. The effect of so large an annual distribution among this class would be to diffuse, in a few years, competence and happiness where now exist only poverty and misery. [13]

The new prosperity envisioned by Kellogg is not a function of usurious economic growth, but rather of the "distribution" of capital through low-interest loans widely among the population.

Kellogg, it should be clear by now, envisions a very different kind of money from that with which we are familiar: ". . . if money were properly instituted and regulated," he tells us,

> there would never be such a thing as a money market. There would be a market for the productions of labor; and these would doubtless vary more or less in their market value or price, but there would be no variation in the market value of money. It is as unreasonable for people to gain great wealth by fluctuations in the market value of money as it would be for them to gain great wealth by fluctuations in the length of the yard. Money is as much a standard of value as the yard is of length; and deviations in the market value of money are as much a fraud upon the public as deviations in the length, weight and size of other measures. No matter how long this gross wrong has been practiced upon all nations, it is no less an evil; and it has shown itself to be such by the centralization of wealth in every nation, and the poverty of the people whose labor has produced the wealth. [14]

Kellogg intended his fixing of the value of money at 1.1 percent to be a universal law, with no one anywhere, ever, including banks or governments, allowed to charge more than 1.1 percent for money loaned out. He writes of banks "closing up their business," but being allowed nonetheless the full value of their assets, insofar as "no injustice will be done to them, for the law making paper money [Safety Fund notes] a tender in payment of debts, gives to it a value equal to that possessed by gold and silver money regulated at the same rate of interest. While the establishment of the Safety Fund can do no wrong to the banks, it will greatly benefit those engaged in production and distribution."[15] Kellogg refers here to the specie-backed banks of his day, but his argument applies just as well to the fiat money of Federal Reserve notes in today's banking system. Capital under his system would become cheaply and widely available at local public credit banks to anyone with good collateral, *and not otherwise.* Kellogg had a strict standard for collateral (it had to be land); how far that might be adjusted for current conditions, if at all, is an open question. Students, for instance, perhaps on parents' collateral if not their own, might take out public credit loans instead of student loans. Public credit banks might offer 1.1 percent interest credit cards. Homebuyers might take out public credit loans instead of mortgages. Small businesses (sole proprietorships and partnerships) might take out public credit loans instead of borrowing money from commercial banks.

Kellogg is not explicit about the identity of borrowers except to describe them occasionally as farmers or artisans, but he speaks throughout only of individuals and citizens, not corporations or governments. In Kellogg's world the latter presumably would not be able to borrow from public credit banks as he conceived them. Given the central role both play in today's world, however, and their need for credit, it is hard to see how they could or should be excluded from the public credit system, provided their financial needs could be made consistent with and subordinate to it, and that the abuses of unrestrained corporate and governmental power which have accompanied the development of modern society are fully addressed. However large enterprises and big government might be reformed and restructured—corporate "personhood," for instance, might be abolished, and governments made more accountable—they would have to play by the same credit rules as everyone else; indeed access to low-interest credit, based on their good collateral, might serve them well. Large enterprises and governments have a vital role today, but in a sustainable, steady-state economy they would presumably be very different beasts from the minimally accountable, profit-maximizing behemoths so familiar to us today.

A centralized national currency, as we have today, would be replaced in Kellogg's system by a locally-issued but still national currency. All the public credit notes would be identical, no matter which local bank issued them. All would be interchangeable and of uniform value everywhere. In all places they would be subject to common national standards, including the low, fixed 1.1 percent interest rate, ensuring that each local public credit bank reliably issues equivalent units of currency; we might call these units public credit dollars. A dollar issued by one local public credit bank, Kellogg intended, would be worth the same as and be freely interchangeable with one issued by any other. The independence of local branches would be guaranteed by the discretionary power reserved to them exclusively to actually create money as loans on the basis of collateral. The compatibility of their monies would be ensured under federal law, above all, by fixing the value of the dollar by law at 1.1 percent/year, that is, by lending money to citizens at that fixed rate everywhere, but at that rate only. Kellogg's system is designed for local control of capital and resources: "The Safety Fund," he tells us, "will lend money at a low rate of interest to all applicants furnishing the requisite landed security; hence every town, county, and state, which has the power to perform the necessary labor, can make internal improvements without pledging its property to large cities or to foreign nations to borrow money."[16] It is the people in every town, county, and state, those who labor and produce, that Kellogg is talking about, not large corporations or large governments. He was a Jeffersonian minimalist not only about government (like many who call themselves conservatives today) but also about corporate power; his goal was economic (as well as political) decentralization.

The amounts of money lent in Kellogg's system would vary considerably from place to place, with some areas needing and creating more currency than others. Larger amounts would naturally be loaned out and put into circulation in areas with large commercial and industrial enterprises. The solvency of local federal public credit banks would be guaranteed by the collateral pledged for their loans, and the money supply would be stabilized by repayment of loans as they came due. Since fixed-rate, non-usurious loans would not be leveraged, deposits in public credit banks would be held in full, and always be fully available. As money is continuously created through new loans, it is continuously extinguished by their repayment. The interchangeability of public credit bank notes would ensure a wide circulation for the new money. Kellogg's public credit banks can be understood as a form of free banking, but done as a regulated non-profit public service rather than as an unregulated and unstable private for-profit enterprise.

The profound implications of Kellogg's money system cannot be overstated. There would be NO controlling central bank in the modern sense, and NO discretionary central issuance of currency by behind-the-scenes decisionmakers, or anyone else, to privileged borrowers. The banking system would be set on its head. A bottom-up system of capital creation by demand would replace the old top-down system. Most fundamentally, credit would be made available to the general public at a perpetually fixed, stable, and sustainable 1.1 percent interest rate on good collateral, instead of being made available selectively to large commercial banks at higher rates, who in turn lend it at their discretion to others at even higher rates—all in a usurious spiral benefiting creditors and impoverishing debtors. With interest eliminated as a factor in monetary policy, the principle engine of wasteful and compulsive economic growth—the forced repayment of loans in excess of their natural value in production and consumption—would be eliminated. There would be no need to labor frenetically and destructively to overcome the interest burden. Economic investment could be initiated on the merits of the situation alone, not on a legal obligation or contract to meet an abnormally forced rate of return. A sustainable economics would become possible, for the first time since the pre-industrial age. And, not least, the widespread availability of capital to individuals (unknown since the closing of the Western frontier in America in 1890, when it was available in the form of land) would do much to overcome the vast and growing discrepancies of wealth which exist because of usurious interest rates.

With the radical decentralization of economic decision-making proposed by Kellogg's monetary system, the principal mechanism for the concentration of capital—a centralized, monopolized, usurious financial system—would be eliminated. Credit would be widely and freely available to anyone with reasonable collateral. It would be as available in rural as well as urban areas, and dollars issued in any place would be fully interchangeable with dollars issued anywhere else in the country. The benefits of borrowing money would no longer go disproportionally to creditors, but would be reserved to borrowers. Concentrations of wealth would persist, naturally enough, but they would be due to successful enterprise, not to the accumulation of interest on debt. More importantly, they could no longer be perpetuated by passive investment in high-yielding debt instruments. The wealthy would have to invest in tangible assets—real estate, equities, etc.—whose value would be tied to the real economy, not to speculation, and their wealth would fluctuate accordingly. This elimination of instruments for the artificial concentration of wealth would help ensure the broader distribution of capital. Kellogg's system is perfectly compatible with free enterprise—indeed it would promote it by leveling the financial playing field. It would introduce a stable currency pegged to the productive potential of borrowers, and would thereby facilitate trade and commerce, domestically and internationally. The dampening of speculation—rooted in usurious interest rates—would rationalize finance and economics, removing much of the cause for "irrational exuberance."

Kellogg's model of a decentralized but democratically regulated monetary system is worth pondering not only for financial and economic reasons, but for political ones as well. Democracy is necessarily a decentralized, face-to-face affair; it cannot be successful unless its citizens personally enjoy relative economic independence in a relatively decentralized economy. Only then can they come together as equals in a free community. Providing capital directly to the people in this way promises, over time, to reduce in large part if not eliminate economic inequality. Most citizens today, by contrast, are economic dependents, having been forced into debt servitude by usurious interest rates for most of the necessities of life (education, housing, transportation, etc.). Not being free economic agents, they cannot easily oppose the harsh and destructive economic system which oppresses them, nor the policies of those who control it. A key step in making possible greater political freedom is the realization that a decentralized, self-regulating, non-usurious monetary system—of the sort outlined by Kellogg and advocated in part by Greenbackers and Populists and others in the later nineteenth century—can provide the basis for widely distributing and conserving wealth, making possible a more sustainable and fulfilling way of life. If the current usurious system is ever to be unwound and replaced with something like Kellogg's system, it will have to be in the context of a broader return to the Jeffersonian tradition of decentralized political and economic power, a tradition which found its last full flowering among late nineteenth century American populists. The increasing dysfunctionality of our centralized economic and political structures suggests that a devolution and dispersion of power to local communities may come about whether we like it or not. Although the Jeffersonian tradition has been eclipsed for many decades by the triumph of big business and big government, we are fortunate to have its precedents available to us, if we are wise enough to utilize them, in any future political restructuring.[17]

In the meantime, one may be tempted to dismiss Kellogg's ideas as remote, even utopian. Kellogg was no idle dreamer, however, but a practical man who made his own way in the world; he was raised on a farm, largely self-educated, and successful in business. He took the long view and refused to conclude that the current unlikelihood of ideas otherwise compelling was a fatal disqualification. Let us give him the last word:

> It may be admitted that the theory of the Safety Fund is good, but impracticable at present; it is calculated for some future generation, when men shall have become more intelligent and virtuous. If the same faith shall be held by the generations which are to follow us, it will be difficult to point out at *what* period this desirable reformation will occur, because the evil of our present system will always be in the present, and the good of the plan proposed in the future. We are, however, persuaded that a large majority of the people are aware that their present depressed condition may and should be exchanged for something better, and the safety Fund will be regarded by them as neither too Utopian nor visionary to be made immediately operative for their benefit. All the objections to the proposed currency, upon the ground that it will lessen the incomes of capitalists who are supported by the labor of others, only serve to show the true working of the Safety Fund system; for its object is to furnish a standard of distribution which will cause men to sustain such mutually just

relations as to render it generally necessary for all to render an equivalent in useful labor for the labor received from others. [18]

NOTES

1. For a firsthand account of the victory of "the money power" over the populist-Jeffersonian tradition, see R. F. Pettigrew's *Triumphant Plutocracy: The Story of American Public Life from 1870 to 1920* (New York: The Academy Press, 1923).

2. Lause, Mark A., *Young America: Land, Labor, and the Republican Community*, Urbana: University of Illinois Press, 2005, p. 122.

3. See the essay by Chester McArthur Destler, "The Influence of Edward Kellogg upon American Radicalism, 1865-1896," in his *American Radicalism, 1865–1901* (Chicago: Quadrangle Books, 1966), pp. 50–77.

4. Edward Kellogg, *A New Monetary System: The only Means of Securing the Respective Rights of Labor and Property and of Protecting the Public from Financial Revulsions*, [1861], (reprint New York: Burt Franklin, 1970), p. 274.

5. Ibid., p. 276.

6. Ibid., p. 286.

7. Ibid., p. 289.

8. Ibid., p. 279.

9. Ibid., pp. 61–2.

10. Ibid., p. 138.

11. Ibid., p. 266.

12. Ibid., pp. 184–5.

13. Ibid., p. 192.

14. Ibid., p. 230.

15. Ibid., p. 302.

16. Ibid., p. 307.

17. I explore the themes of this paragraph at length in my book, *Fixing the System: A History of Populism Ancient & Modern* (New York: Continuum books, 2008).

18. Kellogg, *A New Monetary System*, p. 306.

Chapter Eight

Understanding Money

The essence of modern money, I have been arguing, is debt, not exchange, though any monetary system normally fulfills the latter function as well. That modern money—as invented in the financial revolution—is fundamentally debt is a fact missed or side-stepped by many commentators. One of the early exceptions was Frederick Soddy, an astute British monetary theorist of the 1920s. He puts it well when he says money "is a token certifying that the owner of it is a creditor of the general community and entitled to be repaid in wealth on demand."[1] He expands on this insight:

> Money is not wealth even to the individual, but the evidence that the owner of the money has *not* received the wealth to which he is entitled, and that he can demand it at his own convenience. So that in a community, of necessity, the aggregate money, irrespective of its amount, represents the aggregate value of the wealth which the community prefers to be owed on these terms rather than to own. This negative quantity of wealth I term the *Virtual Wealth* of the community because the community is obliged, by its monetary system and the necessity of having one, to act as though it possessed this much more wealth than it actually does possess.[2]

We have had two kinds of money in history: commodity money and debt money. Soddy is speaking about the latter, not the former. Before the financial revolution of the seventeenth and eighteenth centuries, the idea that debt (bills of exchange and other notes and IOUs) could be money was for most people at best incompletely recognized. Money to most people in most places since the dawn of history has meant commodity money, principally precious metals, and especially silver and gold. Such token monies as existed—from Sumerian temple accounts to bills of credit at medieval fairs to English tally sticks—remained subordinate to commodity money; they could predictably and relatively quickly be directly converted into commodity money if necessary. Perhaps most important, the possibility of a convenient conversion was largely taken for granted. Commodity money in circulation, mostly coins minted by one sovereign or another who gave it his or her stamp guaranteeing its purity and authenticity, remained limited by the availability of precious metals. As we have argued, since such metals had an intrinsic and widely recognized value, any exchange in which they were used to buy goods and services was immediately reciprocal and fully discharged: the seller receiving gold and silver got something directly in return *equivalent* to what he or she surrendered to the buyer. Wholesale merchants, by contrast, buying and selling over long distances with reliable partners needed credit, and credit might be extended locally as well, but these remained special arrangements discharged rather quickly (rarely more than seasonally), with a clear frame of resolution. Debts were generally short term; there were few if any mechanisms for perpetuating debt indefinitely, or automatically renewing it. The standard of money remained a valued coin, and these came to circulate widely in the later Middle Ages, as they had under the Roman Empire. Coins, to repeat, had the advantage of closing rather than prolonging a transaction.

Token money, in contrast to commodity money, allows the reciprocity of exchange to be deferred; it turns the potential buyer who holds the token into "a creditor of the general community," as Soddy puts it, whose claim can *later* be satisfied. Commodity money allows and needs no such deferral; since it is real wealth it automatically closes any transaction. Commodity money is a medium of exchange, but it is *not* itself an instrument of debt, though debt can be denominated in commodity money. Gold and silver and similar commodities, such as precious gems, can function as more or less universal commodities, widely desirable and convenient in their ability to be transported and exchanged for almost anything else. But, as universal items of exchange, they do not transcend the barter system; rather they rationalize and perfect it. Traditional commodity money, from the perspective of modern debt money, remains a kind of proto-money, that is, not yet fully realized money. Only with the financial revolution of the seventeenth century did fully-realized money develop, and only then did large-scale credit become possible, though it was fatefully shackled, as we have seen, by the imposition of usury.

The long history of commodity monies created a mindset that money is above all a medium of exchange, an assumption still deeply rooted today in the public mind in spite of the steady replacement of commodity monies with token monies over the last three hundred years. The movers and shakers of the financial revolution—goldsmiths, investors, brokers, traders, speculators, bankers, etc.—all knew better. But it was not in their interest then—any more than it is for their successors today—to trumpet the insight that money is a token of debt rather than an actual commodity. What those in the know would rather not advertise is that, as a token, money in circulation is no longer fixed by its supply, by some external constraint, as are commodity monies, and that its quantity now is determined by little more than the discretion and reputation of the issuing authority. It is quite one thing to mine gold, transport it, refine it, mint it, and put it into circulation as coin. It is quite another to print paper money or authorize bookkeeping entries (loans) to create deposits at banks. The former is a laborious process of material production of a more or less scarce resource; the latter is a virtually effortless gesture, an act as simple as a stroke of a pen or the click of a key. The former quickly comes up against physical limitations; the latter can be replicated almost effortlessly and endlessly. Commodity monies cannot be expanded or contracted, except with considerable difficulty. Token monies, however, know virtually no limits; the quantity of these tokens can range freely from zero to infinity. (Both, we might note, are fiat monies insofar as they enjoy the imprimatur of the monarch or state which gives them an exclusive legal standing as official media of exchange.)

The long, slow shift from commodity money to token money is a shift from a naturally occurring currency to an intentional currency, that is, to one existing by the will of an issuing authority free of any encumbrance. A commodity currency is commonly issued officially by the sovereign or some comparable authority, but this need not mean more than standardizing the unit used and adding the authority's stamp verifying the purity of the gold or silver; the gold or silver without the authority's stamp are in principle just as valuable and just as much a currency, if less convenient and more subject to challenge. A token currency, however, consists *only* in the issuing authority's stamp of validity, and is free of any natural value or limitation. This has been true of the United States dollar, for instance, since President Nixon withdrew from the international gold standard in 1971. Since it is issued by command—whether by a government or a banking system—token money is often identified with fiat money. I use "token" rather than "fiat" to describe this new kind of money in order to emphasize its debt nature, that it is a ticket or claim on resources, as Soddy points outs, and in consideration of the fact that commodity monies can also be fiat monies, when stamped by a sovereign. The recognition that token money could be issued in quantities far beyond what any commodity currency would allow is the key to the seventeenth century financial revolution. It was a secret first grasped by the goldsmiths, it seems, when they discovered that their depositors could be counted upon not to simultaneously withdraw their deposits; this allowed them, as everybody knows, to safely lend out amounts far exceeding their deposits in the form of tokens, or gold certificates, payable in gold on demand, since normally only a small fraction of such certificates would ever be cashed in at any one time. They discovered that they could create money which would not otherwise exist through lending—we now call it fractional reserve banking—considerably in excess of their deposit base.

Fractional reserve banking is a kind of middle ground between pure commodity money, involving no indebtedness at all, and pure token money, involving nothing but debt. Most of the world has been functioning on pure token money since the international gold standard finally collapsed in 1971. But earlier, during the three hundred years it took us to move from dominant commodity monies at one extreme to pure debt money at the other, a kind of umbilical cord still held connecting money to precious metals, even if ever more tenuously. That cord was stretched thin as less and less collateral or backing by precious metals was needed for the money in circulation, their place being taken more and more by the *promise* of future production of goods and services, a promise made more plausible by the reality of continued economic growth after the eighteenth century. The collateral backing for money was shifted via indebtedness, in other words, from specie and other things actual and present to things future and increasingly hypothetical. We can never reach the point where all collateral is future rather than present; that would be a kind of theoretical limiting case—a fantasy economy, not a real one. However, we can and have gone so far beyond any actual collateral so as to mortgage most of the value of our money many times over—to the tune of hundreds of trillions of dollars—to a future which now seems unlikely to be realized, which looks more and more like a fantasy.

When the U.S. dollar, the world's reserve currency at the time, was taken off the international gold standard in 1971 we arrived at a point where the fractional reserve principle was severed from any lingering connection to precious metals and applied generally and vaguely to the economy as a whole. In other words, instead of gold and silver backing the monetary system, the economy itself—specifically its anticipated output of goods and services, and especially the underlying resources enabling production, including oil above all—became the basis of money; and just as traditional banks lent out on the security of the specie in their vaults, just so the central banks (the Federal Reserve, among others) now lent out both to the government and to private banks on the basis of how the economy was likely to do. A growing economy means that the government can collect more taxes, ensuring that the money it borrowed from the Fed could be counted upon to be repaid with interest. It also means that money borrowed through the privatized financial system and relent to corporations and the public will more likely be repaid with interest. A contracting economy means the opposite.

The recognition that there ought to be some kind of base or collateral for token or debt money is no more than the recognition that debts must sooner or later be repaid, that a token received in payment for goods and services can hold its value only if in due course it can actually be redeemed for an equivalent value in goods and services. The great virtue—and vice—of token currencies is their elasticity: they allow us (that is, those in authority) to adjust very broadly how much debt we are willing and able to take on. With the commodity currencies of the past, by contrast, we were forced to pay for everything, or most things, out of current or near-term cash flow because all exchanges had to be discharged if not immediately than rather quickly by an equivalent amount of real value: gold or silver or some similar more or less convenient and in-demand commodity of value. One cannot as easily go into excessive debt, particularly long-term or perpetual debt, with a commodity currency as with a token currency.

This means that we cannot count on issuing enough of a commodity currency to pay for capital projects and other enterprises (most notably, wars) requiring large up-front sums of money. Individuals who already have money can lend it out, of course, as has been the case since recorded history began, but a commodity monetary system is too inflexible and its currency too scarce to allow for large-scale, reliable debt financing. It cannot drive an economy, or even sustain it. When the goldsmiths and other financiers discovered in the seventeenth century that they could issue tokens (gold certificates) as currencies far in excess of their collateral base, they opened the door to an unprecedented expansion of the monetary system, and thereby to economic growth, though it took centuries for this insight to sink in fully and become widely accepted. This new-found ability to finance production more or less at will was an extraordinary discovery, one with huge promise for improving (as well as endangering) the human condition.

It did improve the human condition, dramatically and spectacularly, for a time. Resources were exploited as never before and living standards rose for the bulk—if not all—of a rapidly expanding global population. But this progress was uneven, wealth and power were concentrated not distributed, and resources were exploited and depleted, not renewed, in the process, leaving us over-extended. If token money, once invented, had been made the basis of a monetary system which made credit available to all, without extraneous and arbitrary extortions attached, resources might have been developed not only renewably but equitably. Overshoot might have been avoided, and a population adequate to its resources might have been maintained. As it was, however, a privatized debt-compounding financial system superimposed upon any useful debt the extra burden of usurious interest, sending us, we can now see, spiraling out of control. In an economy expanding more quickly than the current rate of interest, even usurious rates will be worthwhile for borrowers, provided they can put the borrowed money to work for an even greater return. But if the economy cannot be made to produce enough goods and services—real wealth—to keep up with the increasing obligations which must be paid off in the future, then at some point the system becomes insolvent and debts must be liquidated by default. When investors realize that the game is up, confidence disappears and the system collapses, as in 1929 and 2008.

Most monetary critics do not fully understand the usurious debt money system. Reformers, especially progressives, commonly complain that the problem is the private rather than public nature of credit, and that if the fiat monetary system were truly under government control (as it was with Civil War Greenbacks and earlier colonial currencies) then, they say, it could be managed responsibly for the public good rather than irresponsibly for private interests. This approach stops well short of transforming the existing system. Its essential feature—usurious interest—is preserved, only now it becomes a tool of government finance instead of private accumulation. These reformers are preoccupied more with the concentration of wealth in private hands—which they seek to break down and spread out—than with the evils of usury as such. The principal strategy of progressives, liberals, and others on the left has been to call for some kind of monetary system run by the government rather than Wall Street. But as long as debt is issued by a central authority it is hard to see how this enormous power can be controlled; it is certainly doubtful and perhaps naïve to believe it can be used for public benefit by so-called "democratic" governments as we know them, insofar as they remain largely enthralled to special interests. Even non-usurious lending by a central authority can easily be abused; the temptation to issue debt—without rigorous standards of collateral for repayment, as Kellogg insisted upon—can be overwhelming, after all, with inflation and possibly hyperinflation the result.

The reformers of recent decades, who have favored replacing our privatized monetary system with a public system, go back in part to a group of dissident, non-Keynesian economists in the 1930s led by Irving Fisher, who hoped to reintroduce something like the Greenback system, but failed to persuade the powers of the day to do so. Other advocates of reformed centralized public finance appeared during that era, taking somewhat different tacks. Alfred Lawson led a movement calling for "direct credits" to replace the private financial system. Perhaps more well-known was the social credit movement led by Major C. H. Douglas, influential in Canada, Australia, and New Zealand; a more recent variant is the Basic Income Guarantee (BIG), an idea taken seriously by Richard Nixon.[3] The idea behind these various efforts was to have the federal government directly issue a token currency in payment of its obligations, bypassing the private financial system. This approach is also the focus of Stephen Zarlenga's *American Monetary Institute*, which advocates 1) nationalizing the Federal Reserve to issue "modern American Greenbacks," as he puts it, 2) ending fractional reserve banking in favor of 100 percent reserve banking (to prevent the continued private creation of money by banks through loans), and 3) instituting "anti-deflation programs," mostly public works projects in the New Deal mode.[4] The money supply would be regulated by a federal monetary authority, empowered to set targets for issuing money to balance inflationary and deflationary pressures.

It is hard to see how in Zarlenga's system adequate credit could be made available to the public. Banks would charge interest on their loans, but being unable to engage in fractional reserve lending, they could make relatively few loans. Although Zarlenga allows for the government to lend to banks, there is no provision for direct government loans to individual citizens. Like most progressives, Zarlenga recognizes and appreciates the power of debt, and is aware that modern money is not merely a medium of exchange, as it is under a gold standard, but, as Soddy made clear, that it is also a debt held against future production. The difficulty he and other progressive reformers have had is in disentangling interest from usury. Unable to clearly separate the two, they leave the line between them inevitably blurred, effectively providing a cover for usury. They also underestimate the exhaustion of the debt potential by previous excess borrowing and the eco-crisis of resource scarcity and rising costs. Paul Krugman, for instance, in recent columns in *The New York Times,* calls for greater deficit financing and a replay of the New Deal, downplaying the fact that we are maxed out on debt today: personal, corporate, and government debt in the 1930s and 1940s was miniscule by comparison.

Zarlenga remains unclear to what degree modern money is debt (when in fact it is virtually 100 percent debt). He thinks his greenbacks would be "debt free" money, yet any token currency issued by the government to pay its bills is as much a claim against future production—and therefore a debt to be repaid—as any other kind of token money. Progressives like Zarlenga display a unwarranted faith in centralized power. A nationalized Federal Reserve or other central money-issuing authority can be no better than the accountability to which it is subject. Unfortunately, just such accountability has been woefully lacking in the U. S. federal government and most modern national governments, and particularly so in financial matters. Money put into circulation through payment for government contracts, on the model of the Greenbacks, presents obvious opportunities for abuse. The very idea of a centralized monetary authority issuing currency is a recipe for economic tyranny. The temptation to charge usurious interest on the issuance of money might prove hard to resist, particularly in times of crisis.

Another progressive critic of privatized finance, Ellen Hodgson Brown, adopts most of Zarlenga's points. She goes on, however, to call for a "network of banks to serve as local bank branches of the newly-federalized banking system," such a network being "authorized to service the credit needs of the public." This sounds like Kellogg until she adds: "Interest on advances of the national credit would be returned to the Treasury to be used in place of taxes."[5] When asked in an interview what can be done about our "malfunctioning system," she responds as follows:

> . . . if the money is issued publicly by a public entity, a public bank like the colonial Bank of Pennsylvania, . . . the interest goes back to the public. Instead of having this parasitic system where you have a wealthy class that is living off money making money, the profits or the interest would go back to serve the people themselves. It could be used for more loans, it could be used to defray taxes, it could be used for public good instead of private speculation.

She goes on to describe the kind of public bank she and many other reformers have in mind: "They would be creating money for themselves. Basically they'd be doing the same thing that the private banks do, but they'd be doing it better. They'd be doing it for the people instead of for the bankers."[6]

This anticipated benevolence seems unlikely, however, and the faith put in it somewhat innocent. The power to commit usury, absent further conditions, far from being prohibited is hereby transferred from the private to the public sphere. A central issuing agency—whether a central bank or the Treasury Department—is key to the progressives' vision. The Kelloggian idea that issuance ought to be a local not a state or national prerogative is conspicuously missing. The potential for abuse in a top-down system is high. Rates would remain variable, and there is no limit to what rates a government dependent on interest income might charge. In Kellogg's system, by contrast, interest is not only fixed at 1.1 percent to benefit borrowers, but lending is exclusively reserved to borrowing by individuals *with good collateral*. It is not a substitute for taxes, as it is for Brown and other progressives. Substituting interest for taxes would virtually guarantee the continuation of usurious rates. That they would now be set by government apparatchiks rather than private bankers would hardly be encouraging.

Along similar lines to Zarlenga and Brown, the ideas of Irving Fisher and the Chicago School of the 1930s have recently been revived by Jaromir Benes and Michael Kumhof in a 2012 working paper for the International Monetary Fund entitled "The Chicago Plan Revisited." The original Chicago Plan developed by Henry Simons and others during the Depression "envisaged the separation of the monetary and credit functions of the banking system, by requiring 100 percent reserve backing for deposits."[7] The idea is that money would be issued as fiat currency by the government instead of through loans by the private banking system. With 100 percent reserve backing for deposits, private banks would lose their powers of leverage and speculation. Since the government would issue money directly to pay its bills instead of borrowing it from the banking system, government debt would be reduced; private debts, they theorize, would also be reduced since money would be put into general circulation by government expenditure rather than through private borrowing.

The idea of a government-issued, non-interest bearing currency seems a promising one, but once more the faith put into centralized monetary creation seems misguided. Benes and Kumhof admit that there "have been historical episodes where government-issued currencies collapsed amid high inflation," but these episodes, they say, are so "unrelated to the fact that monetary control was exercised by the government, that they need not concern us here." The lessons of these episodes, they add, are not to start a war, and not "to put a convicted murderer and gambler . . . in charge of your monetary system."[8] The last reference is to John Law. Unfortunately, the propensity of governments to start wars is far from extinguished; nor can we be confident in an age of unmitigated political and financial corruption that some new John Law might not find himself with the power to dispose of a national fiat currency. Kellogg sought to preserve a stable currency by decentralizing its issuance, eliminating usury, and providing uniform standards of local lending. He specifically avoided a government fiat currency, with all its potential for corruption, and insisted on locally issued loans on good collateral—a far different thing—as the basis for a national currency.

Nothing in the original or revised Chicago Plans precludes usurious interest rates on lending out the government's fiat currency once it is in circulation. Moreover, the temptation remains for governments to introduce usurious lending for its own benefit, as suggested by Ellen Brown. Should that occur, should interest become a source of income for governments, they will be not only in a position to extort high rates, but to direct spending where they wish. A largely unaccountable central government, such as we have had in the United States for many decades now, at least since the Civil War, would almost inevitably be tempted to use its power to issue money to favor its clients, not the general good. And, to repeat, bad enough as usurious rates are, even low, non-usurious lending by the government without democratic control or stringent criteria of collateral and other standards of credit-worthiness, remains a recipe for disaster.

Although we are nowhere near the kind of state capitalism many progressives envision, we have seen the American government, in the wake of the crash of 2008, becoming—on the backs of taxpayers—the lender of last resort, taking limited ownership shares in troubled banks and other private corporations, such as General Motors. These attempts, however, like FDR's before them, were aimed to preserve the private usurious system of debt, not overthrow it. Under the ongoing reign of the Federal Reserve System the private banks continue to be able to regulate themselves; proposals to eliminate usury are nowhere to be seen. Under the direction of Treasury Secretaries Henry Paulson and Timothy Geithner and Federal Reserve Chairman Ben Bernanke, it would appear that the banking system has—at least in the short run—expanded its power in the wake of the crisis. It has now managed to appropriate to itself direct access to the capital of tax revenues, thus taking out a new lease on life. Whether the system can survive in the long run remains to be seen. The fact is that the "money power" continues to call the shots in the meantime, effectively controlling state and federal governments through lobbying and campaign contributions. The current arrangement, if it survives—and it may not—will continue to prop up the privatized system, and is likely only to postpone, not avoid, a day of reckoning where genuine not pseudo reforms, and perhaps a transformation of the system itself, might become possible.

A more radical version of centralized government control of the monetary system can be found in the communist states of the twentieth century. Communists were clearer than progressives about the evils of usury, which they did not tolerate. Like progressives they tended to confuse usury with debt, but unlike them they concluded that if usury is bad, so is debt. Although central banks in the Soviet Union and other communist countries provided credit to state enterprises, such credit, though non-usurious, proved far too limited. It was advanced conservatively, on the basis of existing rather than anticipated resources, in a kind of throwback to the days when commodity monies were dominant. Even worse, ordinary citizens had no or little access to credit. Central planners set prices and allocated production quotas, working through large, bureaucratized state enterprises. Those enterprises in turn exchanged many resources through large-scale bartering, settling their accounts on a cash basis. Beyond their inability to utilize large enough amounts of credit, the classic communist command economies, as in the Soviet Union, in the absence of viable markets with accurate pricing structures lacked reliable feedback about demand, consumption, preferences, etc., resulting in inadequate information for decision-makers at the top. Consequently, shortages in some areas and wasteful overproduction in others created bottlenecks, gluts, scarcities, and inefficiencies sufficient to produce a chronically dysfunctional production system, especially with regard to consumer goods. There were few effective penalties for poor performance in communist countries; nobody went bankrupt. "We pretend to work," as the old Soviet joke had it, "and they pretend to pay us." Lack of personal ownership of assets ensured a general apathy with regard to resources, and a rigid one-party political system marginalized dissent, preventing constructive responses to problems.[9]

Communist states provide the best example of full-scale command economies, and of their fatal problems. Command systems might be managed to avoid the compounded debt problems characteristic of usurious societies, but they fail for other reasons. Not only do they avoid compounding debt; they avoid debt in general. The result is an economy starved of capital in contrast to usurious economies which end up drowning in capital, and are gluttons for it. Indeed the latter go so far as to force-feed debt to marginal borrowers. Progressive critics of private usury hope to use state power as a corrective, as we have seen, but tend to ignore the abuses of state power this invites. In seeking to strengthen central monetary authority, progressives (and liberals generally) go down the same road, if not as far as communists. They represent, compared to communists, a hybrid view seeking to balance private property with state power; in most Western countries in recent decades private property and usurious private finance have prevailed over attempts at central state regulation. Should state control over finance someday be established on the model of command economies without corresponding political reform guaranteeing democratic accountability, credit likely would dry up and necessary capital investments would not be made, either by institutions or individuals. It would become very difficult to build a new road or school, or to buy a house or get an education. Capital investments—it cannot be overemphasized—cannot be funded out of current cash flow; they require sums that are available only against the prospect of *future* cash flows. The trick, as Kellogg showed, is to provide credit as needed *without usury and on good collateral.*

One final somewhat speculative possibility for a centralized financial system is the introduction of a new kind of currency based on energy, perhaps through the monetization of carbon credits. Any currency, we have been insisting, needs to be backed by good collateral. In Kellogg's system that collateral was initially defined as land, but could easily be expanded to include any potentially productive resource, including one's own labor. Defining a new currency in terms of energy would discount other forms of widely-held collateral in favor of one privileged form whose ownership and control are already highly concentrated. If our current over-leveraged fiat money system collapses, it could be reconstituted in essentials on the basis of such an alternative energy-based currency. Since control of energy is concentrated in a relatively few large corporations, such a system would likely take the form of corporate-state finance and would likely perpetuate the same usurious abuses we have described with traditional private finance.

The local currency movement—the other widespread response to the current financial system—is radical, not reformist. But unlike communists (or even those who might advocate some new form of corporate-state finance) who are radical about centralizing power, local currency advocates are radical in the opposite direction: they want to dramatically decentralize power. They have little hope that a government-run public monetary and banking system as envisioned by liberals and progressives would be any less oppressive. They distrust big government (as well as big business) and seek instead to eliminate usury by relocalizing monetary functions. Unlike liberals and progressives, they would abolish the heart of the current system: usury itself. But like the communists they repudiate not only the practice of usury but of debt as well, perpetuating the widespread confusion between interest and debt. Debt is so burdened by the abuses of usury in the minds of many radical critics of the current system that they often imagine, it seems, debt itself to be an evil.

The favored alternative financial instruments of the relocalization move-ment are local currencies, perhaps represented best by *Ithaca Hours* in up-state New York and *BerkShares* in western Massachusetts, among many such efforts. This new kind of money for localized, small-scale economies which some imagine will survive a general economic crash is based on the idea that money is above all a medium of exchange—the same assumption made by the command economists and which underlay the old systems of commodity money. This medium of exchange or clearing house model of money is perhaps most fully developed in the work of Thomas Greco, especially in his *Money: Understanding and Creating Alternatives to Legal Tender*, though the idea goes back to Aristotle. Understood exclusively as a medium of exchange, whether by state centralists or localists, money in their view is no more than a neutral placeholder, a token of the value of existing real goods and services, something used above all else to facilitate exchange.

"The ideal money," Greco writes, ". . . should be purely a medium of exchange, and that is what we will consider it to be."[10] "The possession of money," he adds, "should also be evidence that the holder has delivered value to someone in the community and therefore has a right to receive like value in return, or that the holder has received by, by gift or other transfer, from someone else who has delivered value."[11] Notice his insistence that the possessor of money already "has delivered value" or somehow "has re-ceived" value, and so has already earned the money. The door is slammed shut here against the idea that money is debt, as Soddy maintained, that it is not earned in advance but only after the fact.

Indeed, in contradiction to Greco, the creation and issuance of a token unit of circulation is required precisely because *it is not and cannot be coincident* with some prior transfer of value (goods and services). The whole point of credit, as we have seen, is its divorce from direct exchange. What Greco cites as a secondary element in the process—the commitment of the buyer to redeem the currency—is in fact the primary element behind token monies. The borrower agrees to replace the money borrowed, but not neces-sarily to exchange anything. He or she does not part with goods or services in return for a loan; collateral of some sort (perhaps no more than an estimate of future earnings) is indeed pledged, but the borrower, baring default, in the meantime retains that collateral for his or her own continued use. A large enough buyer can in effect create a currency. This is what the federal govern-ment did by printing Greenbacks and using them to pay war contractors during the Civil War. But this harks back toward a command economy, with all its difficulties.

Individual buyers also can create a currency, as Greco suggests with reference to local currencies, but it can be no more than a proto-currency, useful only as a medium of exchange. A medium of exchange currency is a zero-sum game. The limitation of any medium of exchange currency—

whether *Ithaca Hours* or the Soviet ruble—is that it can be issued only up to the value of more or less presently available assets, that is, current goods and services. What is needed, both for individuals and larger entities, is credit which *exceeds*, often dramatically, current assets and the cash flows they produce. As noted above, an individual needs credit to buy a house, get an education, purchase capital items such as a car, etc.; a company or government entity similarly needs credit beyond current assets to make capital investments in machinery, infrastructure, etc. These things cannot be funded by savings or acquired on a cash basis; they must be funded by debt. Otherwise they are and will remain unaffordable.

In sum, radical advocates of centralized government financial systems as well as radical supporters of decentralized local currency movements commonly share a primitive, one-dimensional view of money: they see it not as the inherent debt that it has become, but as essentially a medium of exchange, that is, a clearinghouse instrument. The taint of usury seems to have spoiled, in their minds, the idea of debt itself. The amount of money they are prepared to allow is thereby limited by definition to the value of assets (goods and services) currently available on the market, or more precisely those (like precious metals) that can be spared to function as a currency. Currently available goods and resources are understood to have a value determined by the market; in this view, money can be issued only upon such established value, not on any potential future value. The money-as-a-medium-of-exchange view puts too little money into the system; not understanding that money is debt, it makes no provision for essential capital borrowing.

Command economies of the Soviet type failed because they were starved for investment. If the local currency movement ever became main stream, it would likely fail for the same reason, or act as an obstacle to investment, perpetuating unnecessary poverty. Unlike these radicals, both statists and localists, who tend to fall back into commodity monies, progressives and liberals recognize the importance of debt, though they too fail to distinguish clearly among debt, interest, and usury. This blurring of distinctions reflects the interests of the privatized usurious system. Indeed, most progressives and liberals would nationalize and institutionalize usury. Their position is unstable: the worse the abuses of privatized usurious finance, the more progressives and liberals drift toward state finance and toward incorporating usury in a public monetary system: a recipe for continued debt peonage and political authoritarianism.

The virtue of Kellogg's monetary system in contrast to these inadequate alternatives is that it clearly distinguishes between usury and interest, and repudiates the former and admits the latter. It steers a middle course between the extremes of usury (too much self-multiplying debt) and the strict medium of exchange currencies (too little real debt), and it does so in a way that credit

is locally issued according to national standards and made available to anyone with decent collateral—all in terms of a low, fixed, nominal rate equivalent to the replacement value of goods and services. The curse of too much
credit is the curse of overdevelopment and ruinous and unsustainable economic "growth," while the curse of too little credit is economic contraction
and depression. If we want a steady-state, sustainable economic system we
need a steady-state, sustainable financial system, one which will allow (at
about one percent interest) for the steady replacement of goods and services
as they are consumed.

NOTES

1. Frederick Soddy, *Wealth, Virtual Weal and Debt: The Solution of the Economic Paradox* (London: George Allen & Unwin, 1926), p. 134

2. Ibid., pp. 137–8.

3. See Alfred Lawson, *Direct Credits for Everybody* (Detroit: Humanity Publishing, 1931);
on the Basic Income Guarantee, see the U.S. Basic Income Guarantee Network: http://
www.usbig.net/whatisbig.html.

4. See Stephen Zarlenga, *The Lost Science of Money: The Mythology of Money; the Story
of Power* (Valatie: The American Monetary Institute, 2002), pp. 665, 674; see also website of
The American Monetary Institute: http://www.monetary.org/.

5. Ellen Hodgson Brown, *The Web of Debt: The Shocking Truth About Our Money System—The Sleight of Hand That Has Trapped Us in Debt and How We Can Break Free* (Baton
Rouge, Third Millennium Press, 2007), pp. 461–2.

6. Ellen Brown, "Web of Debt: The Global Money Trap & How We Can Break Free,"
interview with *Acres U. S. A.*, April 2010, vol. 40, no. 4, pp. 54–63.

7. Jaromir Benes and Michael Kumhof, "The Chicago Plan Revisited," (IMF Working
Paper, August 2012), p. 1.

8. Ibid., p. 16.

9. For a general account of the command system in the Soviet Union and its limitations, see
Nikolai Shmelev and Vladimir Popov, *The Turning Point: Revitalizing the Soviet Economy* (By
Nikolai Shmelev and Vladimir Popov. London: Tauris. 1990), *et passim*.

10. Thomas J. Greco, Jr., *Money: Understanding and Creating Alternatives to Legal Tender*
(White River Junction, Chelsea Green Publishing Co., 2001), p. 24.

11. Ibid., p. 25.

Index

agriculture, 21, 56, 66, 82
AIG. *See* American Insurance Group
American colonies, 50, 83–84
American Insurance Group (AIG), 92
American Monetary Institute (Zarlenga), 118–119
American Revolution, 83
annuities, 67; in Netherlands, 34, 40
Armitage, David, 53
Ashton, T. S., 66
Asian financial crisis (1990s), 87
austerity, 9, 86

bankers, 32
bank notes, 35, 47
Bank of Amsterdam (Wisselbank), 38, 45, 50
Bank of England, ix, 86; as corporation, 46–47; credit and, 2, 45–47, 48; establishment of, 23, 51, 53; shareholders in, 52
banks: commercial banks, 9, 68, 87, 109; industrial revolution and, 66–68; 100 percent reserve banking, 118, 120; public credit banks, x, 98–110; reserves of, 16. *See also* central banks; fractional reserve banking; *specific banks*
barter system, 16, 54
Basic Income Guarantee (BIG), 118
Benes, Jaromir, 120
BerkShares, 124

Bernanke, Ben, 121
BIG. *See* Basic Income Guarantee
bills of credit, 64
bills of exchange, 35, 54
Black Death, 31, 32
bonds: government bonds, 9, 47, 67, 81, 88; The Safety Fund, 102
Bonney, Richard, 48
boom and bust cycle, 7, 63, 70, 83–86
Bouton, Terry, 83–84
Brewer, John, 40, 48–49
Britain: agriculture in, 21, 56, 66, 82; American colonies and, 50, 83–84; credit in, 3, 49–51, 56, 63, 65–71; debt at end of Napoleonic wars, 3, 8; financial revolution in, 1, 12, 21, 45–54, 56; France compared to, 67; industrial revolution in, 3, 61–62, 64–71; *laissez-faire* economy of, 86; loan defaults in, 32–33, 54; national debt in, 47–48, 51, 54, 65, 86; Netherlands' relationship with, 40, 46, 50; South Seas bubble in, 53, 70–71; taxation in, 46–47, 49; usury in, 22, 23, 29n10. *See also* English system
British consol (perpetual annuity), 67
Brown, Ellen Hodgson, 119–120, 121
bubbles: dot-com bubble, 87; Mississippi bubble in France, 70; South Seas bubble in Britain, 53, 70–71; tulip bubble (1630s), 38

Bibliography

Anderson, B. L., and Cottrell, P. L. *Money and Banking in England: The Development of the Banking System 1694–1914*. London: David & Charles, 1974.

Andrade's, A. *History of the Bank of England 1640–1903*. [1909] 4th ed. New York: Augustus M. Kelley, 1966.

Anonymous. *Diary of a Very Bad Year: Confessions of an Anonymous Hedge Fund Manager*. New York: Harper Perennial, 2010.

Arbitrage, David. "The Projecting Age: William Paterson and the Bank of England." *History Today*. 44.6 (1994): pp. 5–10. Platinum Periodicals, Proust. Web. Nov. 2009.

Ashton, T. S. *The Industrial Revolution: 1760–1830*. London: Oxford University Press, 1968.

Bagehot, Walter. *Lombard Street: A Description of the Money Market*. London: John Murray, 1922.

Baker, Jennifer J. *Securing the Commonwealth: Debt, Speculation, and Writing in the Making of Early America*. Baltimore: Johns Hopkins University Press, 2005.

Baleen, Malcolm. *The Secret History of the South Sea Bubble: the World's First Great Financial Scandal*. London: Fourth Estate, 2003.

Barnes, Peter. *Capitalism 3.0: A Guide to Reclaiming the Commons*. San Francisco: Berrett-Koehler Publisher, 2006.

Benes, Jaromir, and Kumhof, Michel. "The Chicago Plan Revisited" IMF Working Paper, Research Department, International Monetary Fund, August 2012.

Bentham, Jeremy. "Defense of Usury" [1816] In *The Works of Jeremy Bentham*, ed. John Bowring. Vol. 3, New York: Russell & Russell, 1962.

Bernstein, Peter L. *Against the Gods: The Remarkable Story of Risk*. New York: John Wiley and Son, 1996.

Bouton, Terry. *Taming Democracy: The People, the Founders, and the Troubled Ending of the American Revolution*. Oxford: Oxford University Press, 2007.

Braudel, Fernand. *Capitalism and Material Life: 1400–1800*. Trans. Miriam Kochan. New York: Harper and Row, 1967.

Brewer, John. *The Sinews of Power: War, Money and the English State, 1688–1783* Cambridge: Harvard University Press, 1988.

Briys, Eric., and De Varenne, Francois. *The Fisherman and the Rhinoceros: How International Finance Shapes Everyday Life*. New York: John Wiley & Sons, 2000.

Brown, Ellen H. *The Web of Debt: The Shocking Truth About Our Money System—The Sleight of Hand That Has Trapped Us in Debt and How We Can Break Free*. Baton Rouge: Third Millennium Press, 2007.

Cantor, Leonard. *The Changing English Countryside: 1400–1700*. London: Routledge and Kegan Paul, 1987.

Catton, Jr., William R. *Overshoot: The Ecological Basis of Revolutionary Change*. Urbana: University of Illinois Press, 1982.

Clanton, Gene. *Congressional Populism and the Crisis of the 1890s*. Lawrence: University of Kansas Press, 1998.

Clapham, Sir John. *The Bank of England: A History*. Vols. 1 and 2. Cambridge: Cambridge University Press, 1945.

Clark, Gregory. *A Farewell to Alms: A Brief Economic History of the World*. Princeton: Princeton University Press, 2007.

Coggan, Philip. *Paper Promises: Debt, Money, and the New World Order*. New York: Public Affairs, 2012.

Cipolla, Carlo M. *Before the Industrial Revolution: European Society and Economy, 1000–1700*. New York: W. W. Norton, 1976.

Cohen, Joel C. *How Many People can the Earth Support?* New York: W. W. Norton, 1995.

Collins, Michael. *Banks and Industrial Finance in Britain 1800–1939*. Cambridge: Cambridge University Press, 1991.

Commons, John R. *Institutional Economics: Its Place in Political Economy*. Madison: University of Wisconsin Press, 1959.

Cottrell, P. L. See Anderson, B. L.

Crouzet, Francois. *The First Industrialists: The Problem of Origins*. Cambridge: Cambridge University Press, 1985.

Davies, Glyn. *A History of Money from Ancient Times to the Present Day*. Cardiff: University of Wales Press, 2002.

Davis, Josuha, "The Crypto-Currency: Bitcoin's Mysterious Inventor." *The New Yorker*, 10 October 2011

De Varenne, Francois, see Briys, Eric.

Debt and Economic Renewal in the Ancient Near East. Eds. Michael Hudson and Mark Van De Mieroot. Bethesda: CDL Press, 2002.

Destler, Chester McArthur. *American Radicalism 1865–1901*. Chicago: Quadrangle Books, 1966.

Diamond, Jared. *Guns, Germs, and Steel: The Fates of Human Societies*. New York: W. W. Norton, 1997.

—. *Collapse: How Societies Choose to Fail or Succeed*. New York: Viking Press, 2008.

Dickson, P. G. M. *The Financial Revolution in England: A Study in the Development of Public Credit, 1688–1756*. New York: St. Martin's Press, 1967.

Douthwaite, Richard. *The Growth Illusion: How Economic Growth has Enriched the Few, Impoverished the Many and Endangered the Planet*. Rev. Ed. Gabriola Island: New Society Publishers, 1999.

Ehrenberg, Richard. *Capital and Finance in the Age of the Renaissance: A Study of the Fuggers and Their Connections*. Trans. H. M. Lucas. [1928] Reprint, Fairfield, NJ: Augustus Kelly, 1985.

The Federal Reserve System: Purposes & Functions, Board of Governors of the Federal Reserve System. Washington, DC: 1994

Ferguson, Charles H. *Predator Nation: Corporate Criminals, Political Corruption, and the Hijacking of America*. New York: Crown Business, 2012.

Ferguson, Niall. *The Ascent of Money: A Financial History of the World*. New York: Penguin Press, 2008.

—. *The Cash Nexus: Money and Power in the Modern World, 1700-2000*. New York: Basic Books, 2001.

Fergusson, Adam. *When Money Dies: The Nightmare of Deficit Spending, Devaluation, and Hyperinflation in Weimar Germany*. New York: Public Affairs, 2010.

"Financial History of the Dutch Republic," *Wikipedia*, http://en.wikipedia.org/wiki/Financial_history_of_the_Dutch_Republic.

Fisher, David Hackett. *The Great Wave: Price Revolutions and the Rhythm of History*. Oxford: Oxford University Press, 1996.

Fletcher, George P. *Our Secret Constitution: How Lincoln Redefined American Democracy*. Oxford: Oxford University Press, 2001.

Fousek, Ken. See Perry, Geraldine.

Frank, Tenney. *An Economic History of Rome*. [1920] New York: Cosimo Classics, 2005.

Gastmann, Albert L. See MacDonald, Scott B.

Gleeson, Janet. *Millionaire: The Philanderer, Gambler, and Duelist Who Invested Modern Finance*. New York: Simon & Shuster, 1999.

Graeber, David. *Debt: The First 5,000 Years*. Brooklyn: Melville House, 2011.

Greco, Jr., Thomas H. *Money: Understanding and Creating Alternatives to Legal Tender*. White River Junction: Chelsea Green Publishing, 2001.

Greenfield, Sydney. "Making Another World Possible: the Torah, Louis Kelso, and the Problem of Poverty," in *Explore*, September/October 2007, vol. 3, no. 5, pp.. 493–502.

Harreld, Donald J. "The Dutch Economy in the Golden Age (16th–17th Centuries," EH.net, http://eh.net/encyclopedia/article/harreld.dutch.

Heinberg, Richard. *The End of Growth: Adapting to Our New Economic Reality*. Gabriola Island: New Society Publishers, 2011.

—. *The Party's Over: Oil, War and the Fate of Industrial Societies*. Gabriola Island: New Society Publishers, 2005.

Hixon, William F. *A Matter of Interest: Reexamining Money, Debt, and Real Economic Growth*. New York: Praeger, 1991.

—, *Triumph of the Bankers: Money and Banking in the Eighteenth and Nineteenth Centuries*. Montgomery, AL: E-Book Time, 2005.

Hobbes, Thomas. *Leviathan*. Cleveland: Meridian Books, 1963.

Hollis, Christopher. *The Breakdown of Money: An Historical Explanation*. New York: Sheed & Ward, 1934.

—. *The Two Nations: A Financial Study of English History*. New York: Gordon Press, 1975.

Homer-Dixon, Thomas. *The Upside of Down: Catastrophe, Creativity, and the Renewal of Civilization*. Washington, DC: Island Press, 2006.

Horsefield, J. Keith. *British Monetary Experiments, 1650–1710*. Cambridge: Harvard University Press, 1960.

Hutchinson, Frances, et al. *The Politics of Money: Towards Sustainability and Economic Democracy*. London: Pluto Press, 2002.

In Time. Film directed by Andrew Niccol. Regency Enterprises, et al., 2011.

Jenks, Leland H. *The Migration of British Capital to 1875*. New York: Harper & Row, 1973.

Kellogg, Edward. *A New Monetary System: The Only Means of Securing the Rights of Labor and Property and of Protecting the Public from Financial Revulsions* [1861] Reprint; New York: Burt Franklin, 1970.

Kondratieff, Nikolai. "The Long Waves in Economic Life." Trans. W. F. Stolper. *The Review of Economic Statistics*, vol. XVII, no. 6, Nov. 1935, pp. 105–115.

Korowicz, David. *Trade-Off: Financial System Supply-Chain Cross-Contagion: A Study in Global Systemic Collapse*. Metis Risk Consulting & Feasta, www.feasta.org, 30 June 2012, revised.

Kumhof, Michael. See Benes, Jaromir.

Kunstler, James Howard. *The Long Emergency: Surviving the Converging Catastrophes of the Twenty-First Century*. New York: Atlantic Monthly Press, 2005.

Kuzminski, Adrian. *Fixing the System: A History of Populism, Ancient & Modern*. New York: Continuum Books, 2008.

Lachmann, Richard. *From Manor to Market: Structural Change in England, 1536–1640*. Madison: University of Wisconsin Press, 1987.

Lanchester, John. *I. O. U.: Why Everyone Owes Everyone and No One Can Pay*. New York: Simon and Schuster: 2010.

Landes, David S. *The Wealth and Poverty of Nations: Why Some are so Rich and Some so Poor*. New York: W. W. Norton, 1999.

Lause, Mark A. *Young America: Land, Labor, and the Republican Community*. Urbana: University of Illinois Press, 2005.

Law, John. *Money and Trade Considered, with a Proposal for Supplying the Nation with Money* [1705] reprint: New York: Augustus M. Kelley, 1966.

Lazzarato, Maurizio. The Making of the Indebted Man. Amsterdam: Semiiotext, 2011.

Lewis, Michael. *The Big Short: Inside the Doomsday Machine*. New York: W. W. Norton, 2010.

Lipson, E. *The Economic History of England*. 3 vols. 12th ed. London: Adam and Charles Black, 1959.

MacDonald, Scott B., and Gastmann, Albert L. *A History of Credit & Power in the Western World*. New Brunswick: Transaction Publishers, 2001.

Malthus, Thomas Robert. *An Essay on the Principle of Population*. [1826 edition] David Winch, ed. Cambridge: Cambridge University Press, 1992.

—. *The Nature and Progress of Rent*. [1815] Ed. Jacob H. Hollander. Baltimore: Johns Hopkins Press, 1903.

Martenson, Chris. *The Crash Course: The Unsustainable Future of our Economy, Energy, and Environment*. Hoboken: John Wiley and Sons, 2011.

Marx, Karl. *Capital: A Critique of Political Economy*. vol. 1. Frederick Engels., ed. New York: International Publishers, 1967.

—. *Wage Labour and Capital* in *The Marx-Engels Reader*, Robert C. Tucker, ed. New York: W. W. Norton, 1972.

Mathias, Peter. *The First Industrial Nation: An Economic History of Britain 1700–1914*. 2nd ed. London: Methuen, 1983.

Meadows, Donella, et al. *Limits to Growth: the 30-Year Update*. White River Junction: Chelsea Green, 2004.

—, et. al., *The Limits to Growth: A Report for the Club of Rome's Project on the Predicament of Mankind*. New York: New American Library, 1972.

Miller, Joshua. *The Rise and Fall of Democracy in Early America, 1630–1789*. University Park: Pennsylvania State University Press, 1991.

Morgan, E. Victor. *The Theory and Practice of Central Banking 1797–1913*. [1943] New York: Augustus M. Kelley, 1965.

Neal, Larry. *The Rise of Financial Capitalism: International Capital Markets in the Age of Reason*. Cambridge: Cambridge University Press, 1990.

Nelson, Benjamin. *The Idea of Usury: From Tribal Brotherhood to Universal Otherhood*. 2nd ed. Chicago; University of Chicago Press, 1969.

Odum, Howard T., and Odum, Elizabeth C. *A Prosperous Way Down: Principles and Policies*. Boulder: University Press of Colorado.

Orlov, Dmitry. *Reinventing Collapse: The Soviet Example and American Prospects*. Gabriola Island: New Society Publishers, 2008.

Pawson, Eric. *The Early Industrial Revolution: Britain in the Eighteenth Century*. New York: Harper & Row, 1979.

Perry, Geraldine and Fousek, Ken. *The Two Faces of Money*. Shelbyville, KY: Wasteland Press, 2007.

Peterson, William. *Malthus*. Cambridge: Harvard University Press, 1979.

Pettigrew, R. F. *Triumphant Plutocracy: The Story of American Public Life from 1870 to 1920*. New York: The Academy Press, 1923.

Pirenne, Henri. *Medieval Cities: Their Origins and the Revival of Trade*. Trans. Frank D. Halsey. Princeton: Princeton University Press, 1925.

Riegel, E. C. *Flight From Inflation: The Monetary Alternative*. Los Angeles: The Heather Foundation, 1978.

Polanyi, Karl. *The Great Transformation: The Political and Economic Origins of Our Time*. Boston: Beacon Press, 1957.

Polimeni, John M., et al., *The Myth of Resource Efficiency: The Jevons Paradox*. London: Earthscan, 2008.

Reisen, Dominick J. *Middlefield and the Settling of the New York Frontier: A Case Study of Development in Central New York, 1790–1865*. Voorheesville: Square Circle Press, 2009.

Rickards, James. *Currency Wars: The Making of the Next Global Crisis*. London: Penguin, 2012.

The Rise of the Fiscal State in Europe c. 1200-1815. Richard Bonney, ed. Oxford: Oxford University Press, 1999.

The Road. Film directed by Sam Mendes. Dimension Films, et. al., 2009.

Rohe, John F. *A Bicentennial Malthusian Essay: Conservation, Population and the Indifference to Limits*. Traverse City: Rhodes & Easton, 1997.

Runciman, David. "Like Boiling a Frog," review of *The Wikipedia Revolution* by Andrew Lih, in *The London Review of Books*, May 28 2009.

Saint-Simon, Duc de. *Memoirs of Duc de Paint Simon, 1696–1709*. Lucy Norton, trans. Warwick, NY: 1500 Books, 2007.

Schumacher, E. F. *Small is Beautiful: Economics as if People Mattered*. New York: Harper & Row, 1973.

Schumpeter, Joseph A. *Capitalism, Socialism and Democracy*. New York: Harper Perennial, 2008.

——. *History of Economic Analysis*. New York: Oxford University Press, 1954.

Smil, Vaclav. *Energy in Nature and Society: General Energetics of Complex Systems*. Cambridge: MIT Press, 2008.

Sonenscher, Michael. *Before the Deluge: Public Debt, Inequality, and the Intellectual Origins of the French Revolution*. Princeton: Princeton University Press, 2007.

Soddy, Frederick. *Wealth, Virtual Wealth and Debt: The Solution of the Economic Paradox*. [1926] Reprint: Palmdate: Omni Books, 1983.

Solow, Robert M. "Survival of the Richest?" Review of Gregory Clark, *A Farewell to Alms: A Brief Economic History of the World*. in *The New York Review of Books*, vol. LIV, Num. 18, November 22, 2007.

Spufford, Peter. *Power and Profit: The Merchant in Medieval Europe*. New York: Thames & Hudson, 2002.

Tilden, Freeman. *A World in Debt*. Funk & Wagnall's Company, New York, 1936.

Toutain, Jules. *The Economic Life of the Ancient World*. New York: Barnes & Noble, 1968.

Trevelyan, George Macaulay. *The English Revolution: 1688–1689*. London: Oxford University Press, 1938.

Usher, Abbott Payson. *The Early History of Deposit Banking in Mediterranean Europe*. 2 vols. Cambridge: Harvard University Press, 1943.

Vilar Pierre. *A History of Gold and Money: 1450 to 1920*. Trans. Judith White. New York: Verso, 1991.

Vries, J. de, and Woude, A. van der, *The First Modern Economy: Success, Failure and Perseverance of the Dutch Economy, 1500–1815*. Cambridge: Cambridge University Press, 1997.

Weber, Max. *General Economic History*. Trans. Frank H. Knight. Glencoe: The Free Press, 1950.

——. *The Protestant Ethic and the Spirit of Capitalism*. Trans. Talcott Parsons. New York: Charles Scribner's Sons, 1958.

Wilson, Thomas. *A Discourse Upon Usury, by Way of Dialogue and Orations, for the Better Variety and More Delight of All Those that Shall Read this Treatise* [1572]. Introduction by R. H. Tawney, New York: Augustus M. Kelley, 1963.

Wright, Robert E. *One Nation Under Debt: Hamilton, Jefferson, and the History of What We Owe*. New York: McGraw Hill, 2008.

Yelling, J. A. *Common Field and Enclosure in England 1450–1850*. Hamden, CT: Archon Books, 1977.

Zarlenga, Stephen. *The Lost Science of Money: The Mythology of Money—the Story of Power*. Valatie: The American Monetary Institute, 2002.